ALBUQUERQUE
THEN & NOW

ALBUQUERQUE THEN & NOW

MO PALMER

THUNDER BAY
P·R·E·S·S

San Diego, California

Thunder Bay Press
An imprint of the Advantage Publishers Group
5880 Oberlin Drive, San Diego, CA 92121-4794
www.thunderbaybooks.com

Produced by Salamander Books,
an imprint of Anova Books Company Ltd,
10 Southcombe Street, London W14 0RA, U.K.

Library of Congress Cataloging-in-Publication Data

Palmer, Mo.
    Albuquerque then & now / Mo Palmer.
        p. cm.
    ISBN-13: 978-1-59223-655-8
    ISBN-10: 1-59223-655-3
    1. Albuquerque (N.M.)--Pictorial works. 2. Albuquerque (N.M.)--
History--Pictorial works. 3. Historic sites--New Mexico--Albuquerque--
Pictorial works. 4. Historic buildings--New Mexico--Albuquerque--
Pictorial works. 5. Albuquerque (N.M.)--Buildings, structures, etc.--
Pictorial works. I. Title. II. Title: Albuquerque then and now.

    F804.A3P35 2006
    978.9'6100222--dc22
                                    2006050125

2 3 4 5 10 09 08 07

Printed in China.

ACKNOWLEDGMENTS

Special thanks to my mother, Kitty Livingston, who said, "Write a book"; Deb Slaney, Curator of History, the Albuquerque Museum, who read and corrected the entire manuscript; Ed Boles, Historic Preservation, City of Albuquerque; Ann Carson, Huning's Highland Neighborhood Association and the Albuquerque Conservation Association (TACA); Leba Freed, the Wheels Museum; Glenn Fye, Photo Archivist, the Albuquerque Museum; Nancy Ward and Paul Greenberg, Congregation Albert; Terry Gugliotta, University of New Mexico Archivist; Clara Kilcup, Manzano Day School; Lou Liberty, Historian, Sandia Preparatory School; Nick Manole, Yrisarri Building; Loretta Naranjo Lopez, Martineztown/Santa Barbara; Joe Sabatini, Branch Manager, Special Collections, Albuquerque Public Library; and Nancy Tucker, Postcard Collector. Friends, cohorts, and cronies all. I would also like to credit the following sources for providing information for this book: Albuquerque National Bank, *Albuquerque Progress: Business News of Our City*; Charles D. Biebel, *Making the Most of It: Public Works in Albuquerque During the Great Depression*; Lina Fergusson Brown, *Trader on the Santa Fe Trail: The Memoirs of Franz Huning*; Howard Bryan, *Albuquerque Remembered*; Susan DeWitt, *Historic Albuquerque Today*; Erna Fergusson, *Albuquerque*; Elred R. Harrington, *History of the Albuquerque High School, 1879–1955*; Dorothy B. Hughes, *Pueblo on the Mesa: The First Fifty Years of the University of New Mexico*; Byron Johnson, *Old Town, Albuquerque, New Mexico: A Guide to Its History and Architecture*; Bob Dauner and Byron Johnson, *Early Albuquerque, A Photographic History, 1870–1918*; David Kammer, "From Burros to 'Burbs", *Su Casa* magazine (Winter 2003); William A. Keleher, *Memoirs: 1892–1969, A New Mexico Item*; Michael P. Marshall, *A Cultural Resource and Historic Architectural Survey for the Downtown Albuquerque Transportation and Streetscape Improvement Project*; Michael P. Marshall, *A Cultural Resource Survey and Historic Buildings Inventory for the Proposed New Mexico Hispanic Cultural Center*; Mo Palmer, *The Albuquerque Tribune*, Articles, 2000–2006; "Voices of the Past, Oral Histories," the Albuquerque Museum; "Building the Mother Road," NM Route 66 Association; Thomas Arthur Repp, *Route 66: The Romance of the West*; Jeffrey C. Sanders, *McClellan Park: The Life and Death of an Urban Green Space*; Dennis E. Saylor, *Songs in the Night: The Story of Marion Van Devanter*; Diane Schaller, "Compilation, Albuquerque Building Permits, 1913–1937," Historic Albuquerque, Inc.; Sister Blandina Segale, *At the End of the Santa Fe Trail*; Marc Simmons, *New Mexico: An Interpretive History*; *Albuquerque, A Narrative History*; Thomas J. Steele, *Church Buildings and Land in Old Albuquerque*; *Works and Days: A History of San Felipe Neri Church, 1867–1895*; TRC Mariah Associates, Albuquerque Area Archaeology; Marion Woodham, *A History of Presbyterian Hospital, 1908–1976*.

PICTURE CREDITS

The publisher wishes to thank the following for kindly supplying the photographs that appear in this book:

"Then" photographs:
Courtesy Albuquerque Museum, Cobb Collection, Museum Purchase GO Bonds: p. 14 [1990.013.043], p. 24 [1990.013.055], p. 40 [1990.013.002], p. 44 [1990.013.013], p. 46 [1990.013.060], p. 52 [1990.013.029], p. 54 [1990.013.088], p. 58 [1990.013.231], p. 60 [1990.013.014], p. 62 [1990.013.116], p. 108 [1990.013.183]. Courtesy Albuquerque Museum, Milner Studio Collection, Museum Purchase, GO Bonds: p. 20 [1992.005.284], p. 26 [1992.005.120], p. 28 [1992.005.107], p. 56 [1992.005.671], p. 80 [1992.005.517], p. 82 [1992.005.284], p. 86 [1992.005.682], p. 88 [1992.005.500], p. 104 [1992.005.722], p. 106 [1992.005.679], p. 112 [1992.005.688], p. 114 [1992.005.718], p. 118 [1992.005.717], p. 126 [1992.005.649B], p. 130 [1992.005.476], p. 142 [1992.005.509]. Courtesy Albuquerque Museum, Brooks Collection, Gift of Channell Graham and Harold Brooks: p. 30 [1978.151.271], p. 90 [1978.151.856]. Courtesy Center for Southwest Research Collection: p. 18 [1978.050.737], p. 32 [1978.050.075], p. 76 [1978.050.432]. Courtesy Albuquerque Museum, Albuquerque Public Library Collection: p. 98 [1978.141.314], p. 92 [1978.141.102]. Courtesy Albuquerque Museum, Gift of Sytha Motto: p. 38 [1978.077.017]. Courtesy Albuquerque Museum Collection, Ward Hicks Collection, Gift of John Airy: p. 94 [1982.180.507]. Courtesy Albuquerque Museum, Gift of Jacob Johnson: p. 16 [1996.005.004]. Courtesy Albuquerque Museum, Albuquerque Progress Collection, Gift of Albuquerque National Bank: p. 36 [1980.184.757]. Courtesy Albuquerque Museum, Gift of Van Deren Coke: p. 42 [1981.001.016], p. 66 [1981.001.007], p. 68 [1981.001.009]. Courtesy of Albuquerque Museum, Milner Herter Collection, Museum Purchase, GO Bonds: p. 34 [1994.014.069]. Courtesy Albuquerque Museum, Gift of Mickey and Louise Miller: p. 12 [1980.152.003], p. 138 [1980.152.212]. Courtesy Albuquerque Museum, Detroit Photographic Company: p. 22 [1972.042.001]. Courtesy Albuquerque Museum, Gift of Telephone Pioneers Museum: p. 72 [1980.022.003]. Courtesy Albuquerque Museum, Gift of First United Methodist Church: p. 64 [1980.099.002]. Courtesy Albuquerque Museum, Gift of Howard Bryan: p. 78 [1980.100.015]. Courtesy Albuquerque Museum, Gift of Chalmers Pancoaste/Marietta Vorhees: p. 48, p. 74. Courtesy Albuquerque Museum, Gift of Jones/Bonfantine Families: p. 134 [1999.059.004]. Courtesy Nancy Tucker: p. 84, p. 136. Courtesy John Lukens/Eye Associates of New Mexico: p. 116. Collection of Author: p. 132. Courtesy Presbyterian Health Services: p. 120. Courtesy Center for Southwest Research: p. 124. Courtesy Albuquerque Museum, Brooks Studio Collection, Gift of Channell Graham and Harold Brooks: p. 96 [1978.151.999]. Courtesy Albuquerque Museum, Ward Hicks Collection, Gift of John Airy: p. 110. Denver Public Library, Western History Collection, Harry Lake, [L-487]: p. 70. Library of Congress, Prints & Photographs Division, FSA-OWI Collection: p. 10 [LC-USW3-018753-C], p. 100 [LC-USW3-020499-D], p. 102 [LC-USW3-020498-D], p. 122 [LC-USW3-018778-C], p. 128 [LC-USW3-018797-C], p. 140 [LC-USF34-037074-D]. Courtesy Museum of New Mexico: p. 6 [8562], p. 8 [76064], p. 50 [76073].

All "Now" images were taken by Simon Clay (© Anova Image Library).

INTRODUCTION

Albuquerque has been "then" a great deal longer than it has been "now." People may have lived in the area 9,000 years ago. Residential relics dating back to 5500 BC have been found around the city. Ancient cultures come and go and dates are debated, but some things we know. The sophisticated world of the Ancestral Pueblo (formerly Anasazi) in Chaco Canyon, a society with astronomy, irrigation, roads, and elaborate houses, disintegrated around AD 1250, but the reason isn't clear—theories range from drought to enemy invasions. Some migrated to the lower Rio Grande Valley, where water was plentiful and land along the riverbanks was fertile. These ancestors of today's Pueblo Indians settled in this place the Spanish called Tiguex, after the language that was spoken here.

In 1540, lured by stories of "cities of gold," Spanish conquistador Francisco Vásquez de Coronado's expedition reached the pueblo of Zuni. Disappointed to find only cities of mud, Coronado dispatched explorers, still driven by glittering expectations. Hernando de Alvarado went east and saw Acoma Pueblo, gleaming almost 400 feet above the awestruck soldiers.

Alvarado was the first white man to see what would become Albuquerque, with its valley, the Sandia (meaning "watermelon-colored") Mountains, sacred to the Native Americans, its river, and its provision-stocked pueblos. He sent word to Coronado: "Wish you were here, join us for the long winter ahead." Coronado came and a sorrowful story of conquest, struggle, subjugation, and insurrection unfolded over the next 133 years. After the Pueblo Revolt of 1600, a gentler Spain returned in 1693 and a more peaceful coexistence began.

Don Francisco Cuervo y Valdés, temporary governor of the province, informed his superiors in Mexico in 1706 that he had founded the Villa de Alburquerque, named after the viceroy of New Spain, the Duke of Alburquerque. He was being obsequious, as well as bending facts. There were requirements for establishing a villa—more than a mere settlement, with official functions—such as the number of families, a plaza (town square), and a church. Settlers actually lived up and down the Rio Grande, caring for their crops, children, and animals. Eventually, buildings did appear and some may still be seen in the original town, Old Albuquerque. Somewhere along the way, that extra "r" in the name fell out.

Mexico won independence from Spain in 1821, and took over New Mexico. In 1846, the United States took it away from Mexico. Life in the villa went on as usual, centered around church, family, and home. A number of Santa Fe Trail traders, ex-soldiers who stayed after the Civil War, and folks seeking adventure and land drifted in. By the 1870s, Albuquerque was predominantly Hispanic, with some Native Americans, and a few—mostly German—newcomers. But another change, as monumental as Coronado's arrival, loomed.

The railroad reached Albuquerque in 1880. The silver tracks bypassed Old Albuquerque to avoid the frequently flooded Rio Grande and so that rails could be laid in straight lines. A "New Town" bloomed instantly around the depot and shops. New people brought new ways—a different language, Victorian architecture, Protestant denominations, and English legal notions. Cultures would again clash before they eventually syncretized.

The Santa Fe Railway built "the jewel in its crown," the Hotel Alvarado, in 1902, a California Mission Revival–style complex that included arcades, portals, a new depot, and an Indian Building that housed the Indian and Mexican rooms. Attention focused on newly discovered ancient arts. Artists painted ethereal scenes to tempt travelers, and they came—to stay, to purchase beautiful blankets and jewelry, and to watch Native Americans weave right before their eyes. By 1923, Albuquerque had two luxury hotels.

City boosters invited people with tuberculosis to "come to the well country" and heal under cobalt skies, and soon sanatoriums sprouted. After tuberculosis was defeated with antibiotics, many of the resortlike meccas became the full-service hospitals that today underpin Albuquerque's medical economy.

Automobiles and airplanes, which require service and airports, took the railroad's business, and Albuquerque accommodated the new age. Route 66 ran twice through the town—first north and south, then, after 1937, east and west. Motels, eateries, and gasoline stations appeared on every corner. The Mother Road brought mimetic architecture, buildings designed to mimic the goods within. Albuquerque was the "City of Neon" because its signs lit up the sky, beckoning tourists and locals alike. The interstate highways of the 1950s bypassed them all, dooming them to failure and roadsides to a deadly sameness.

Another "invasion" again wrought change. New Mexico's involvement with the atomic bomb and its ancillary technology brought post–World War II scientists to Sandia Laboratories, military personnel to the new bases—Sandia, Kirtland, and Manzano—students to expanded math and science programs at the University of New Mexico, retirees, and ex-soldiers to the pleasant place they enjoyed during the war. Ranches turned into ranch-style homes as developers built flotillas of little houses on the east mesa.

Albuquerque had its troubles. Unorganized growth led to political upheavals; older neighborhoods populated by minorities were neglected and residents became angry; the university erupted in riots over Vietnam and the Kent State shootings. Gradually, people reconciled and Albuquerque became one of the first cities in the United States to enact an equal housing ordinance. Growth never slowed, and the area now has well over 500,000 people.

Albuquerque is, for me, a city of colors. From the sparkling river to the mountains, pink and purple in the afternoon, from adobe walls that shine golden under the blinding sun, creating the illusion of Coronado's cities, to its silver and turquoise adornments and the many flags that have flown beneath its skies. Albuquerque's people are many hues as well, as it is truly a multicultural metropolis. The tiny Villa de Alburquerque has grown into New Mexico's largest city and just celebrated its three-hundredth birthday with hard-earned pride.

Albuquerque was founded in 1706 by Francisco Cuervo y Valdés, temporary governor of New Mexico. At that time all plazas, or town squares, were required to have a Catholic church, but though Cuervo y Valdés fudged figures, claiming he had the required number of settlers to establish a town, the church was not completed until 1719. Without constant attention, adobe bricks will dissolve; the original church (first known as San Francisco Xavier), on the west side of the plaza, melted and fell down in 1792. This is an early photograph of the replacement, erected on the north side of the plaza in 1793. An 1857 engraving suggests that it was built with simpler bell towers. The French Carpenter Gothic steeples were added before Italian Jesuits took over management in 1867.

San Felipe de Neri remains a very active Catholic parish, and since the 1860s the church building itself has undergone remodeling and acquired additions. For example, the original rectory, built on the east side, now has two stories. Over the years, various picket fences and adobe walls have surrounded it. Much time, effort, and money has been invested to renovate the building and maintain its historical integrity, and all of the architects involved have worked meticulously to preserve its character. Regular and special services are still held in the church—it is traditionally packed for midnight mass on Christmas Eve—and while it can be difficult to worship quietly among the tourists, parishioners welcome visitors with grace. In fact, many parishioners from surrounding neighborhoods are descendants of the original settlers.

Sister Blandina Segale was a tiny Italian nun with an indomitable spirit. A Sister of Charity, she was a peppery lady and unafraid of anything—hard work, desperadoes, crossing the dangerous river on a rickety raft, or standing up to anyone with whom she disagreed. In 1880, she and five other sisters came to take over Albuquerque's faltering education program at the invitation of San Felipe de Neri's priest, Father Gasparri. They arrived to find their new home unfinished and were instead obliged to board in rented quarters on the plaza. Undaunted, Sister Blandina found an Italian stonecutter and personally supervised the construction of an unusual two-story adobe building. The convent was completed—and occupied—by 1881.

The convent was built over a cemetery. Locals predicted that because of this, the walls would never stand. When finished, the first floor of the convent, which was named Loyola Hall, held five classrooms while the sisters occupied the small upstairs rooms. Sister Blandina was recalled to Ohio in 1894 and served in several of that state's cities. She died in 1941, after writing her memoirs, *At the End of the Santa Fe Trail*. The Sisters of Charity moved to their new home, St. Vincent's Academy, but returned to the convent residence off and on until the late 1970s. The building has also been used as an infirmary, post office, and school.

New Mexicans were often so poor that children usually had to work alongside their parents in the fields, tend sheep, or help at home. Even late into the twentieth century, many youngsters still left school to help with the harvest. Before New Mexico gained statehood, the wealthy, or *ricos*, sent their sons over the Santa Fe Trail to schools in the United States and girls were not educated at all. Clara Huning, daughter of merchant

Franz Huning, complained that "schools were kept . . . for boys only." In 1881, however, the sisters reopened Our Lady of the Angels, a boys' school built in 1877, and invited girls to attend the public portion of the new school. The nuns taught the three Rs, as well as piano, Spanish, English, drawing, painting, and waxwork. The small cupola above the main door held the school bell.

The Sisters of Charity moved their classrooms to St. Vincent Academy, their school in New Town, in 1887, but the old building stands as testament to their pioneering spirit. Thanks to careful preservation, the Our Lady of the Angels building retains one of the most original appearances of any structure in Old Town today. Since the nuns moved out, the building has housed a variety of shops as well as the Albuquerque Historical Society's museum.

Founded in 1947 as the Old Town Historical Society, its collection of local artifacts was generously donated to the Albuquerque Museum in 1967 and was the foundation of the museum's history division. The parish is justly proud of its heritage and still educates children from prekindergarten through eighth grade.

Manuel Armijo was a short, chubby man and three times governor of the Mexican province of New Mexico. His first gubernatorial term ended with Manuel under suspicion, but he was not to be dismissed easily. In 1837, one of New Mexico's chronic rebellions flared. Armijo led troops to Santa Fe to find the rebels gone. Having inflated his role in their disappearance, Armijo was again appointed governor. When war with the United States broke out in 1846, American forces singing their way to Santa Fe planned to "wallop Fat Armijo." Armijo, meanwhile, led his men to Apache Canyon and then hightailed it back to Mexico, leaving his wife in Albuquerque and New Mexico in American hands. His forty-room adobe mansion stood in Old Town until 1910.

Charles Böttger was an immigrant from Germany who moved to New Mexico for his health. Along with the Sunnyside Inn, west of his home, and a toll bridge over the Rio Grande, he bought Armijo's house; he razed it and built this Italianate/Mediterranean-style home in its place. Several generations of Böttgers lived in "the Mansion" before it was sold to the Garcia family. In the 1940s it belonged to a small community of Buddhists and later it became a boardinghouse. According to legend, Elvis Presley, Frank Sinatra, and Machine Gun Kelly have all visited. The house is said to be haunted, and this has been confirmed by the Ghost Detectives of Los Angeles, who stayed there for a week. They reported at least four ghosts in residence, including the "Old Man," who is assumed to be Charles Böttger himself.

Following American occupation in 1846, Old Albuquerque became a military post. Most of the activity was west of the plaza, between Main Street (Rio Grande Boulevard) and the Rio Grande, though some officers rented quarters on the plaza. Enlisted men lived in barracks. A post hospital, quartermaster's depot, and other buildings were also built to serve the forces, but they have since been demolished and their locations forgotten. The adobe guardhouse was presumably intended for miscreants, but for some reason a barber/dentist set up shop here. The 121-foot-tall flagpole at its center was erected on the order of Post Commander General James Carleton, and was supposedly the highest west of the Mississippi. It was taken down in 1900, thirty-three years after the military left town.

Over the years, the center of the plaza has hosted many functions. After the old guardhouse was knocked down, a wooden bandstand was built; older residents still remember the music of locally famous bands and dancing on the wooden floor that was put down for the evening. Despite the bandstand's popularity, in the 1930s a Works Progress Administration project put men to work building a replacement stone wall and gazebo. The wall and gazebo were not well received, and one of the first tasks of the fledgling Old Albuquerque Historical Society was to get rid of them. Thanks to them, music is still played in the current bandstand and dancers perform. The bandstand is traditionally covered with *luminarias* or *farolitos* (little lights) for Christmas Eve. San Felipe Church hosts an annual fiesta in honor of San Felipe Neri, the village's patron saint.

This is Ambrosio Armijo's (nephew of Manuel Armijo) store and house, built between 1876 and 1881. It was originally two square buildings joined by a walkway. The railroad brought new building materials and new architectural styles to New Town, and allowed residents of Old Town to anglicize their homes, hence the wooden facade. Inside is a magnificent walnut staircase that leads up to a small area. Legend says that Ambrosio built it so his daughter could make a grand entrance in her wedding gown, though recent research indicates that the dates of its building and her marriage do not coincide. This photograph, taken some time later, shows the Steuckel-Johnson family, part of the German merchant community, who rented the house in 1896.

Old Town retained its rustic charm and family-oriented community while all around it New Town frenetically expanded. For many years this part of town was not considered a good business investment, and early pioneers were unable to borrow money to establish businesses here. Nevertheless, stores and restaurants gradually appeared, and Old Town has now become a tourist destination, featuring some of the oldest buildings in the country as well as unique arts and crafts. Armijo's home and store became a tea room in the 1940s, and now serves New Mexican and American food while Native American vendors sell their unique arts and crafts on the shady portal. The property has been bequeathed to the Albuquerque Museum Foundation.

Herman Blueher was a German immigrant who arrived in Old Town as a lad of nineteen and began working as a farmhand. Over the years he amassed enough money to buy his own "truck farm," which grew produce that was then "trucked" around town and sold to housewives and stores. Blueher built this Queen Anne–style brick house in 1898. Inside were etched glass doors and a separate staircase for servants. The farm's fields once occupied land that is now the Albuquerque Museum and Tiguex Park, while Blueher's Pond, a recreational site, was an irrigation depression stocked with fish. Its outline can still be seen at the northeast end of the property. Although the farm may be long gone, many of Herman Blueher's descendants still live in the area.

The Blueher House was intact as recently as 1950, but after it became La Hacienda Restaurant, the house was "puebloized" and the entrance set at an angle to the plaza. The second story is just visible, though its roofline is now flat. However, in the parking lot behind the building, much of the original house can still be seen. Herman Blueher's fields became Tiguex Park in the 1970s. Recently, the park was massively remodeled and has stone entrance gates that pick up the architectural details in the new museum addition to the west. To celebrate Albuquerque's 300th anniversary in 2006, Tiguex Park was renamed Tricentennial Tiguex Park.

People lived here before Albuquerque was founded in 1706. The area was called Hacienda de Doña Luisa de Trujillo. Luisa inherited the property when her husband died. Existing residences were destroyed during the Pueblo Revolt of 1680, when the native Pueblo peoples united against the Spanish. This house, southeast of the plaza, may have existed before the revolt or been built later, but regardless, it is very old. During the Civil War, occupying Confederates slaughtered animals under this cottonwood tree—the blood is said to have contributed to its enormous size. Franz Huning, who traded on the Santa Fe Trail, bought it in the 1850s and named it La Glorieta. Here he brought his bride, Ernestine. The original building was L-shaped, but Huning enclosed two sides to create this *placita*, or courtyard.

The Huning family lived here until Franz built Castle Huning across the street in 1883. He gave La Glorieta to his daughter Clara and her husband, Harvey Butler Fergusson, whose children were noted Southwestern authors Erna and Harvey Fergusson. It remained a private residence until the 1930s, when Ruth Hanna McCormick Simms, concerned with education, started the Sandia School for Girls and then the Manzano Day School for younger children. Both schools, at different times, operated in La Glorieta. Manzano Day School, a private school for kindergarten through fifth grade, occupies the site today. Every effort was made to save the old cottonwood tree, but it was cut down in 1984 because it was diseased and administrators feared it would fall. The courtyard is still lovely and inviting, as shown in this photograph.

A successful, wealthy merchant and a city father, Franz Huning built this mansion as a Christmas present for his family in 1883. The castle in the desert stood between Old Town and New Town, symbolically connecting the two. It was constructed of *terrones*, or sod bricks dug from the river bottom, and painted to look like wood. Some say Huning copied a German castle; others claim that it was an Italianate villa. Whichever country provided inspiration, it was a grand house, with a tower, a ballroom, and two inside baths, quite a novelty in the 1800s. Huning's land extended to the south and west, and the house's grounds boasted a pond, an arboretum, grapevines, and gorgeous gardens. A sign over the front door proclaimed it "Castle Huning."

Franz and Ernestine Huning lived in the castle until their deaths; their son, Arno, lived there until the 1920s, after which it was divided into apartments. For a time it became a school, but by the 1950s government offices occupied the castle. Unfortunately, the once-beautiful house had deteriorated and by 1955 the fountain and yards were shabby and choked with weeds. Castle Huning was demolished. All that remained was an empty lot. Recently, the Huning Castle Apartments opened and the original fountain (pictured here) was restored to its rightful place. Huning's gardens and vineyards are now part of the Albuquerque Country Club.

For much of the nineteenth century, Bernalillo and Albuquerque battled to be the county seat. Bernalillo prevailed in 1878, but in 1883 the honor was returned to Albuquerque, creating the need for a decent courthouse. New Town and Old Town both vied to become the site of the important offices, and the internecine fighting raged for several years. Both sides filed legal documents, but Old Town raised a larger fund and was awarded the coveted honor of erecting the building. Fortunately, talented stonecutters were among the first Italian immigrants to arrive in the city and in 1886 Palladino and Bernardinelli created this three-story cast-stone building. For years, folks came here to pay taxes and conduct business. In 1926, however, a new courthouse was built in New Town. The old courthouse was retired and sold to the San Felipe de Neri Church.

The San Felipe de Neri School opened in the vacant courthouse in 1927 and remained there until 1959. Some alumni recall it as a rather scary place, with daunting stone steps leading up to the entrance and dark woodwork inside. Despite some public outcry, the old courthouse was demolished in 1959 for reasons that are still unclear and a new school was constructed in a different location. The school is still active and serves students from kindergarten through eighth grade. This playground is all that remains of the old site.

The South Valley is a group of very old Hispanic plazas—Armijo, Atrisco, Los Padillas, Pajarito, and others. Atrisco was founded before Albuquerque, and the Atrisco Land Grant organization is still active today. The South Valley remains part of Bernalillo County and resists annexation by the city, fearing for its charming rural culture. Originally, county schools comprised an independent district, but a poor one because of the agricultural tax base. The goodness, guts, and determination of administrators and teachers kept the district afloat. Many recall purchasing supplies out of their own pockets. Designed by educator Atanacio Montoya, the Armijo School opened in 1914. It served the village of Armijo until 1948, when a new school was built.

A new Armijo Elementary School opened nearby on Gatewood Road and it is now part of the Albuquerque Public School District. The old building continued to stand, but it deteriorated until it was purchased by Bernalillo County. The one-of-a-kind little redbrick schoolhouse has now been fully restored. Today it is used as a community center, meeting hall, and, recently, as Nuestros Valores, an alternative charter school for ninth through eleventh graders who do not thrive in a traditional school environment. The old Armijo School has also been designated as a local and national landmark.

Though today tamed and shallow, the Rio Grande in the past could become a raging torrent that swallowed people, livestock, and homes. When it flooded, residents often had to grab what they could and head for the hills. At other times, when the water was low, locals could hoist up their skirts and trousers and wade across. A variety of bridges—including a pontoon—were built across the river and washed away over the years, but the best crossing was at the oxbow in the Hispanic plaza of Barelas. The 1912 steel bridge was adequate until tourist traffic on Route 1 and then Route 66 became too heavy and a stronger one was needed. This rare 1920s photograph shows a new cement bridge alongside the old one.

The original Route 66, created in 1926, came south from Santa Fe, through Albuquerque and Barelas to Isleta Boulevard, following El Camino Real, the original "Royal Road" between New Spain (Mexico) and its northern province of New Mexico. At the village of Los Lunas, tourists headed for California would turn west. By 1928, 3,500 cars were crossing the bridge daily.

Although Route 66 was rerouted in 1937, the older road still carried heavy traffic as Highway 85, the north-south path through the state. Bridge Street now accommodates heavy local traffic between Albuquerque, Barelas, and the South Valley. The eastern part of Bridge Street is now César Chávez Boulevard, named in honor of the farm workers' rights campaigner.

Henry Ford's cars made touring possible to people who had previously never been able to afford travel. Some carried cots on their running boards, and many passengers ate canned food, inspiring the label "tin-can tourists." At first, such tourists were limited in their choice of destinations because America had few roads. Finally, in 1926, the government strung together and numbered a conglomerate of farm-to-market roads, paths, and old trails—one was Route 66.

Tourist camps with gas, water, and food sprouted on the landscape like summer mushrooms. The Napoleone family's Deluxe Auto Camp at Fourth and Bridge was a successful establishment. Indeed, when the city's trolley line bowed out in 1928, the Napoleones bought the old cars for storage. However, someone flipped a firecracker or cigarette into a debris-filled ditch and the fire destroyed all twelve trolley cars.

After Route 66 was rerouted in 1937, many roadside businesses flopped and the land they had occupied was used for other purposes. In 1983, Hispanic leaders formed a corporation to establish a center for arts, education, research, and history. Their dream became reality in 2000 when the beautiful National Hispanic Cultural Center opened on fifty-two acres at the end of South Fourth and West Bridge, including the Deluxe Auto's former space. The center has exhibit galleries, a research library, and the Roy E. Disney Center for Performing Arts, which includes three facilities. There is also La Fonda del Bosque Restaurant, a gift shop, and a genealogy center. The center hosts conferences, history competitions, films, plays, dances, and live music.

Albuquerque was not alone during its first centuries and was not even the earliest or the largest settlement in the area. People settled in other Hispanic plazas up and down the river, seeking fertile land and accessible water for their farms. Los Duranes, Los Candelarias, Los Ranchos, Los Poblanos, and Los Griegos were early towns, not later subdivision developments that were given Spanish names. Plazas were almost always named after their founding family and each hamlet had its own church and patron saint, though not always a priest. The fathers of San Felipe de Neri traveled as frequently as they could to serve the religious needs of these then-outlying areas. Los Griegos was founded as early as the 1700s.

The outlying villages remained viable as the sprawling city began to surround them, though most were not annexed until the late 1940s. The church in the old photograph is now a private home, and the plaza is all but unrecognizable. A new Catholic church has been built, and so have churches of other denominations. Los Griegos is still a village of winding streets, with old traditions, and with property owned by descendants of the early families. The City of Albuquerque has built a public library here, and Los Griegos is part of the Near North Valley Neighborhood Association.

The Spanish had houses and plots of land, but larger tracts were shared for communal grazing. Around 1850, Don Manuel Martín moved his family out to the "sand hills," short dunes that rose between the Rio Grande and the empty plains below the Sandia Mountains, hence the name Martineztown. Presbyterians and Congregationalists, as well as Catholics and others, were prevalent in New Mexico, and the first church in Martineztown was built by Presbyterians in 1889. San Ignacio Catholic Church was built in 1916. People of the various old villages recall that on Easter, after services in their own church, folks walked from plaza to plaza to celebrate with friends and neighbors.

San Ignacio Catholic Church remains a vital parish. It is still an impressive structure with its typical New Mexican corrugated metal roof glittering under the sun and its array of large statues. The long, somber walk up the hill and some of the religious icons have changed over time. A small park is now situated between Edith and Walter streets, running in front of the church, shortening the walk and leaving less room for sculptures. Neighborhood kids are usually shooting hoops there, so it seems to be a positive trade. San Ignacio also serves the Catholics of sister community Santa Barbara and offers an old-fashioned Latin mass at noon on Sundays.

The Santa Barbara School was built in 1908 to serve the children of the Santa Barbara and Martineztown communities. The school started out as a two-room adobe box, but as needs grew, additions were made. According to the New Mexico Board of Architects, between 1908 and 1938 the building gained a peculiar blend of flat and pitched roofs. The Mission Revival–style parapet (the curved facade) was added after 1919, in the style of the Hotel Alvarado, the YMCA, and other local structures. The school stopped operating in 1986, and the city condemned the building.

Residents of Santa Barbara and Martineztown were not ready to see their old school razed. Many local people had fond memories of their days there and the building was a registered landmark that belonged to the City of Albuquerque. Unfortunately, however, the school was in very bad shape after standing vacant for years. Nevertheless, the neighborhood fought city hall and won. The school was renovated and re-created as eight accessible apartments for low-income seniors with disabilities. Office space and a community meeting room were also added. The new Santa Barbara Apartments opened in 1992. The exterior looks new today and the neighborhood can be proud to have saved a piece of its history.

The Atchison, Topeka, and Santa Fe Railway (AT&SF) originally selected Bernalillo, a village ten miles north of Albuquerque, for its terminal and shops. However, Don José Leandro Perea, who owned the land and operated a freighting business, asked for $425 per acre. So railroad officials, accustomed to acquiring land for two dollars an acre, headed south—and Albuquerque's destiny was determined. To avoid flooding and so that straight tracks could be laid, the original town was bypassed and a mile and a half to the east, New Town was born. This 1881 photograph shows the depot beside the tracks, with a view north to empty land. The small shack on the right is on the intersection of the tracks and Railroad Avenue.

New Town grew outward from the railroad tracks and Railroad Avenue, which was renamed Central Avenue in 1907. Soon the intersection was the hub of the tiny city, with wool warehouses, a scouring plant, a flour mill, wholesale houses, and a brewery, as well as hotels and restaurants to accommodate the ever-increasing passenger traffic on the Santa Fe.

Although buildings have come and gone, this remains the gateway to downtown Albuquerque. On the right is the restored Springer Transfer Company building. On the left is the parking structure for the Albuquerque Convention Center. Cars head under the tracks next to the Alvarado Transportation Center, a replica of the Hotel Alvarado.

As New Town developed by the railroad tracks, its architecture reflected the efforts of newcomers from the East and Midwest to reproduce their familiar hometowns. The building on the corner of Front Street (First) and Railroad Avenue (Central) is Hope's European Hotel, later the Sturges Hotel. This was a "perhaps house"—railroad towns across the West boomed and busted, so some edifices were prefabricated and rode the rails as a need arose. This one lived in two other towns before planting its roots in Albuquerque. The horse-drawn streetcar carried riders between Old Town and New Town, sometimes stopping while a lady bought a hat or a gentleman ducked into a saloon. Electric trolleys replaced the horse-drawn streetcars in 1904.

The Sturges Hotel, Whitney Hardware, and other buildings on South First Street gradually fell into disrepair and were demolished. This block remained empty and served as a parking lot until the city's ten-year downtown revitalization program started to change the face and image of the area in the late 1990s. The architectural firm of Moule & Polyzoides held a design *charrette*—an architectural brainstorming session. Using archival photos, a new block was created, with details that reflect those of the original buildings. Now a multiplex theater, restaurants, New Mexico Business Weekly, and other enterprises fill the space and invite people to return downtown. Subtle details on the facades suggest the Victorian ambience of a previous time.

The railroad reached Albuquerque in 1880, and for fifty-seven years pedestrians and vehicles stopped at this crossing of Railroad Avenue and the tracks to wait until trains clattered by. The Highland Hotel, a frame and brick structure, offered the "European" plan, or rooms without meals, perhaps as a less-expensive alternative to the Hotel Alvarado by the depot.

The Highland went out in a spectacular blaze of glory when it burned in 1905. As liqueurs in the saloon ignited, spectators were treated to Chartreuse, crème de menthe, absinthe, and other colored fireworks. Farther up the avenue are the homes of prominent newcomers, with the tower of the library and academy visible on the left.

During the Great Depression, an influx of New Deal dollars enabled Albuquerque to build an underpass to eliminate the gridlock created by passing trains. The Hudson Hotel, seen here on the right, was built in 1905 to replace the demolished Highland Hotel. Designed by architect Francis W. Spencer, the building is one of the few Richardson Romanesque–style buildings remaining in the city. The top two floors hosted guests, particularly the many traveling salesmen, or "drummers," who passed through on the Santa Fe Railway. Commercial enterprises operated on the first floor, with its recessed display windows. The Hudson was preserved and renovated in the 1980s and now serves as office space.

Albuquerque's first "luxury" hotel was the Armijo House at Third and Railroad. Built by Mariano Armijo (Ambrosio Armijo's son) in 1881, it was frame and adobe, with a fancy French mansard roof, and was soon an important building. New Town was built on a "yazoo," or swamp, and an *acequia* (irrigation ditch) ran through the middle of town. So that ladies didn't muddy their long skirts on the way to the hotel, there was a boardwalk from the railroad depot. Gentlemen were required to don coat and tie to enter, unusual in a frontier town, and at least one bout of fisticuffs resulted from a disagreement over appropriate dress. Frame structures look pretty but burn quickly, and in this land of little water, the hotel was ashes by 1897.

A second Armijo Building was erected almost as soon as the Armijo House burned down. Sanborn Fire Insurance maps show it as a hardware store by 1902. It was referred to in city directories as the "New Armijo Building" until the 1910s. The Army Recruiting Center was housed upstairs. Downstairs was Mandell's, a business that had several partners over the years but continued to serve the city. In 1917, it sold dry goods, clothing, ladies' ready-to-wear, and shoes. As Mandell and Dreyfuss, the store offered "men's and boys' furnishings and shoes." This old building was remodeled more than once. It now has an ordinary facade but an interior courtyard reveals some of the older structure.

The San Felipe Hotel on the southwest corner of Fifth and Gold was Albuquerque's second luxury hotel and a three-story eleganza that rivaled the Armijo House. It cost $103,000 to build and had eighty rooms that rented for between $2.50 and $3.00 per day. The San Felipe even had a separate entrance for ladies, so they wouldn't have to smell cigar smoke as they walked through the lobby. According to historian Marc Simmons, one promoter, Colonel Meylert, was a teetotaler and rigidly moralistic. Instead of a bar, he installed a reading room. In no time at all, the hotel failed—perhaps a reflection of popular culture of the time. Like its counterpart, the Armijo House, the building yielded to flames, in 1899.

The Benevolent Order of Elks organization picked up the singed pieces of the San Felipe and opened a theater, where plays, music, and even Albuquerque's opera star, Claude Albright, appeared to packed houses nightly. Single Elks members lived upstairs. Later, the structure was enlarged to accommodate more members and was known as the Elks Lodge. A stuffed elk was displayed outside for many years. In 1964, the lodge sold the building to the government. The building was razed and the thirteen-story Dennis Chavez Federal Building was erected, named for the Albuquerqeuean and beloved New Mexico senator. When a new post office and courthouse were built, these functions moved out, but many agencies remain.

Albuquerque loves a parade. Although the occasion being celebrated here is unknown, we can assume it was one of New Mexico's many hoping-for-statehood celebrations. New Mexico remained a territory of the United States until 1912, as it was viewed almost as a foreign country—Spanish speaking and predominantly Catholic. The Rosenwald brothers were German merchants who arrived in 1878 and opened a store in Old Town. Shortly after the railroad arrived in 1880, they moved to this store in New Town. Later the family would construct the first reinforced concrete building in the city. Two early buildings are visible, the N. T. Armijo Building behind the telephone pole and the Zeiger Building behind it.

The eight-story First National Bank was Albuquerque's first skyscraper, built in 1922 by Trost and Trost, distinguished architects from El Paso, Texas. It replaced the old bank at Second and Gold, which began as Central Bank, moving from Old Town to New Town with the railroad's advent. This cathedral of commerce cost $585,000. The interior features marble counters, high arched windows, and brass appointments, making it one of the city's most elegant structures. Doctors, lawyers, and other professionals maintained offices upstairs. The building was utilized for banking until First National moved to the Galeria in the 1970s. It is now being renovated for use as loft apartments.

This is West Gold Avenue between Front (First) Street and Second Street around 1895. The little burg by the railroad tracks had grown considerably. Victorian-styled buildings included, from right to left, the post office—with a poster for a performance at the Grant Opera House (which later burned) in its window—Western Hardware, Wells Fargo, a furniture store, the Knights of Pythias Hall, and the YMCA. Secret societies were hugely popular in the late 1800s and early 1900s. A perusal of almost any early city directory reveals Shriners, Knights of Columbus, and, in Albuquerque, the Oriental Order of Humility. Many had ladies' auxiliaries. Most of these buildings survived into the second half of the twentieth century, when they fell to urban renewal.

In early Albuquerque, single people and families lived downtown, above stores and businesses, in centrally located boardinghouses, in second- and third-story walk-up hotels over retail establishments, and even in the finer hotels, the Alvarado and the Franciscan. After the streetcar and automobile made suburbs possible, downtown living was left to denizens of flophouses and the impoverished. Now downtown living is once again popular. These are the Gold Street Lofts, which have refilled the empty land left by the demolition of the old structures.

Albuquerque has always been an extremely multicultural place. The "tricultural city"—Native American, Hispanic, and Anglo—is a myth. Although "Anglo" means "English," it has become synonymous with "white-skinned," but Germans, Italians, Greeks, Asians, and many others populated Albuquerque from the beginning. Indeed, Germans settled in Old Town before New Town even existed. This photograph shows the Bryant Company Delivery Service at 222 West Gold Avenue around 1913. General N. Bryant, an African American, owned the business. His descendants are still here. In the background is the Walter G. Hope Building. Built in 1894, the structure housed Dr. Hope's medical office and his home. George Albright's printing press was on the first floor. Albright's wife, Franc, was a photographer.

Somehow these buildings escaped the wrath of renewal. Modern businesses here include the Patrician Design/Caliente It's Hot! gallery, which features art ranging from paintings to fabrics. The trendy Gold Street Caffè attracts visitors and downtown workers with a menu that includes everything from a "hearty cowboy breakfast" to healthy salads. Edith Cherry and D. James See have their architectural firm in Dr. Hope's old building. The firm works on many of the city's preservation projects. Other stores and offices also occupy these old structures. With growing trees and obviously well-maintained facades, this revived block clearly offers a positive sign for historic preservation and for downtown revitalization.

Four financial institutions occupied the four corners of West Gold Avenue and South Second Street, giving rise to the sobriquet "Bankers' Corner." Large buildings such as this were often referred to as "blocks." Oliver Cromwell established the horse-drawn streetcar line, the Albuquerque Street Railroad, and in 1882 built this block. The old Albuquerque National Bank, not affiliated with a later bank of the same name, was located here until a scandal arose in 1893 when the bank defaulted and its president was indicted. At one time, the building belonged to General Douglas MacArthur's wife. Washburn's, a popular clothing store, was an occupant for many years.

The Cromwell Block was razed during urban renewal and a vacant lot took its place. The downtown revitalization program finally filled up the many vacant lots created by the urban renewal of the 1970s. This building's corner architecture obviously mimics the old Cromwell Block, as the architects drew upon archival photographs in their design. Although only one building covers the space between First and Second streets, its design incorporates subtle features of the old building and creates the illusion of Victorian decor. It also appears that the smaller businesses still occupy the block, which makes the area seem familiar. The Greater Albuquerque Chamber of Commerce now occupies part of this building.

Charles Zeiger built this structure in the 1890s. It originally housed Quickel and Bothe's, the "finest restaurant in the Southwest." However, it was also a saloon that advertised "the finest whiskies, imported wines, and cognacs" as well as cigars. The striking cupola on the roof is half-fake, as the two backsides do not exist. Zeiger's closed in the 1910s due to Prohibition, and probably because of Albuquerque's 1907 ban on gambling. The State National Bank of Albuquerque operated here until it folded in 1924. The building was then turned over to Albuquerque National Bank, founded by George Kaseman, who served as president from 1924 until 1938. The original building was extended with matching architecture that made the addition appear seamless.

In 1956 the Albuquerque National Bank decided that it needed a new building and set about construction in an original way. Part of it was built, and everyone moved into it. The Zeiger Building was demolished, and then the south part of the new bank was finished. There is a balcony of sorts across the second floor, from which it is possible to see some of the downtown area. Albuquerque National became Sunwest Bank, then Nations Bank, followed by Bank of America. The bank has moved and the building is now occupied by the Make-a-Wish Foundation and another firm.

Before bicycles and automobiles revolutionized transportation, horses powered local traffic. W. L. Trimble originally owned a livery stable in Old Town, but when he noticed that New Town was growing, he opened a new business on the west side of Second Street in the early 1880s. At Trimble's, one could rent horses, carriages, or one of two behemoth wagons called "tallyhos." The lengthy vehicles carried twenty or thirty passengers and were often used to ferry picnickers to the Sandia Mountains or on other recreational outings. According to historian William Keleher, Trimble also operated a six-horse stagecoach line between several booming mining towns. Eventually, of course, stables lost out to Studebakers and Trimble's closed, although his son stayed in the transportation business, becoming an airline pilot.

Conrad Hilton was born south of Albuquerque. His parents ran a store and an inn of sorts, where young Hilton learned the hotelier trade. Albuquerque's own Hilton Hotel, which opened in 1939, was his fourth hostelry. It was here that Hilton and Zsa Zsa Gabor announced their engagement. The Hilton was a hangout for politicians, who sometimes paged themselves to appear popular. The hotel features Native American murals, Spanish vigas, tin chandeliers, and arched doorways. When Hilton needed more space, the building was sold and became the Hotel Plaza. Caught in downtown's slide toward flophouses, the landmark was almost lost, but a timely grant from the city restored its original beauty. Reopened as La Posada, it is advertised as "the small hotel of historic proportions."

Early Albuquerque depended on volunteer firemen. Three "hose companies" fiercely competed at the annual Territorial Fair. The first paid fire department started in 1900 and is pictured here at its new "firehouse" on North Second Street. There were two men salaried at $60 and $65 per month, plus twenty men on call. The department purchased the volunteers' equipment. Fires were frequent and fearful in this land of little water, and destroyed many structures. When the automobile appeared, buckets of water were placed under the Coal Avenue Viaduct in case an internal combustion engine sparked and set the wood on fire. Every citizen was duty bound, should fire erupt, to start the bucket brigade and extinguish the fire.

The Albuquerque Fire Department soon had better quarters in the new city hall. Different buildings and businesses occupied the general area, including Ange Hardware, Korber's, the Ilfeld Building, and the Angelus Hotel. As downtown declined, great swaths were declared blighted and block after block of old Victorian buildings were razed, particularly along the Tijeras Avenue portion of the project. The new Albuquerque Convention Center, which opened in the 1970s, replaced many of these structures. In the following decades, an eastern complex was added. The western complex contains the Kiva Auditorium, a venue for performing arts. Meeting rooms of all sizes are in the eastern side. Both have recently received some upgrades.

Several Protestant denominations existed in Albuquerque before the railroad arrived in 1880. In 1875, Episcopalians met in a makeshift chapel in a room at the Exchange Hotel in Old Town. The tiny congregation was thrilled to plan for a real church when the town blossomed. They purchased lots at Fourth and Silver and built a small sandstone church. The same material was used for the Atlantic and Pacific railroad shops; some of this sandstone may have been given to St. John's. The doors opened in 1882. Because New Town's population grew rapidly, so did the congregation. According to their history, there was a boardwalk from Railroad Avenue (Central) to the church, so that parishioners could stay relatively clean when walking to services.

The parish continued to grow. In the 1920s, St. John's was designated as the cathedral for this area. A handsome matching building, the Cathedral House, was designed by renowned architect John Gaw Meem. Cathedral House provided space for the new administrative functions. Today, its spaces are devoted to meetings. During World War II, Bishop James Stoney arrived, and he eventually met his goal of making this area a diocese. In 1951, further renovations, again designed by Meem, began on the big cathedral seen here. St. John's has gone from a hotel room to a cathedral, weathered the storms of downtown decline, and still comprises a multicultural congregation. The church also operates Camp Stoney in the foothills outside of Santa Fe.

This is Albuquerque's Methodist Church, a little adobe building at the corner of Third and Lead. The congregation was organized in 1880, and a church soon followed. The small building was replaced in 1904 by a lovely new building with a silver steeple and Tiffany stained-glass windows. It has been a New Mexico Historical Site since 1978. During these beginnings, Methodists were involved with education and health care. Mrs. Thomas Harwood, the wife of a missionary, started a school for girls in 1887. The Methodist Deaconess Sanitarium was built at Pine and Central in 1912. It evolved into Bataan Methodist Memorial Hospital, now part of the Lovelace Sandia medical conglomerate.

The First United Methodist Church decided to remain downtown as many of the neighboring churches moved to Northeast Heights and into the north and south valleys. In the 1950s, a larger worship facility was built, along with an education building, where a preschool and day care was implemented in 1991. The little church with the silver steeple now functions as First United Methodist's Fellowship Hall. Every Monday, the church is open to the hungry, with volunteers serving 250 to 300 meals each week. This "Grace Meal" has been available for eighteen years.

Many Jewish merchants established prominent businesses in Las Vegas, Bernalillo, and Albuquerque, and Albuquerque had an active Jewish population in the late nineteenth century. The religious community, however, had neither a rabbi nor a place of worship. Members of the congregation conducted services at the Knights of Pythias Hall and in their own homes. In 1897, about fifty families came together and effected plans for a place of their own. An auction was held to name the new temple. The Grunsfeld family won with a bid of $250—which was a lot of money in 1897. The name Albert was chosen to honor Mr. Grunsfeld's deceased father. The unique domed building opened in 1900. Congregation Albert moved to a larger facility in 1951.

Temple Albert was sold to the American Legion, although it served other religious functions and wasn't an American Legion post. In 1952, it was the Albuquerque Bible Church and in 1953, the Evangelistic Temple. By 1954, the old domed building was doomed. It was vacant until 1959, when it no longer shows up in city directories and was probably razed. Congregation

Albert, however, thrived, and moved from its "new" 1951 facility to an expanded home in the Northeast Heights in 1984. Today, it includes the temple, a school, a gift shop, offices, and a memorial rose garden. The old site remains an empty lot.

The Commercial Club was both a building and an organization. Founded in 1890, the association of city fathers operated as an early chamber of commerce. Its job was to boost new industries and dwellers, and thereby increase the city's economy. In 1892, their new building at Fourth and Gold opened. There was a billiard parlor, bachelor rooms upstairs, a dance hall, and offices. The club sponsored dances, the annual Bachelors' Ball, and other soirees. The Commercial Club published or financed a multitude of booster booklets that touted Albuquerque as the best possible place to begin anew. After World War I, partying was phased out and the Commercial Club became the Albuquerque Chamber of Commerce.

After the demise of the Commercial Club, its red sandstone building served as French's Mortuary for a time. Then it was purchased by community leaders and brothers John and Albert Simms, and became known as the Simms Building. In 1952, the old Richardsonian Romanesque structure was razed and a new, ultramodern edifice began reaching for the sky, opening in 1954.

Thirteen stories made it the tallest skyscraper in town. Inside were a marble-paneled lobby, a spiral staircase, soundproof offices, and a Panorama Room that provided a full view of the city. Stone blocks from the old building were incorporated as decor on an eastern wall. This new Simms Building was declared a historic landmark in 1988.

The Hotel Alvarado, known as the "jewel in the Santa Fe's crown," opened in 1902. Designed by Charles Whittlesey, with interiors by Mary Colter, it was a California Mission Revival marvel. Portals, fountains, bell towers, courtyards, and gardens combined Spanish and Moorish elements with the work of Native American and Hispanic artists, creating beauty in its halls. It was a destination for tourists seeking the Southwestern exotica extolled by the Santa Fe Railroad, and was the heart of the town. Everyone dressed up to promenade on the brick walk and watch celebrities pass through. Weddings, lunches, dinners, conventions, presidential visits, the glitzy Montezuma Ball—all happened within its walls. Impeccable service was provided by the fabulous Fred Harvey Company, with its Harvey Girls, known as the "Civilizers of the West."

Albuquerque's downtown, like many across the country, declined as suburbs took business to shopping centers and malls. Old bricks yielded to glass and steel towers as urban renewal leveled landmarks. Hotels sat empty while motels were packed. The AT&SF decided to bulldoze the Alvarado. Despite community protest and the city's attempts to buy the property, it fell to the wrecking ball in 1970. The loss galvanized a preservation movement. In 1993, fire destroyed the adjoining railway depot. Parked cars filled the lot until recently, when the Alvarado Transportation Center opened to serve various city transit operations. Although this scene is north of the original buildings, it illustrates the architectural similarity. The complex replicates the Alvarado's architectural details, and the Greyhound station is fashioned after the 1902 depot.

Albuquerque had a struggling telephone service by 1882, started by former territorial governor Miguel Otero Sr. The service had between thirty-four and fifty subscribers. The "horn" did not catch on and subscriptions faded. The Colorado Telephone System bought out Otero in 1887; however, phones still weren't added to many residents' homes. The Mutual Automatic Telephone Company offered competition in 1901, featuring "modern" dial phones.

Unfortunately, subscribers to one service could not talk to those using the other service—those who wished to be able to talk to everyone paid for both services. Period advertisements bragged that the companies had "Both Phones" and listed two numbers. The Colorado Telephone System erected this building in the early 1900s.

The Colorado Telephone Building was surrounded by new businesses. By the 1950s, it was used by the telephone company but its redbrick facade was painted and additional space was added. The Telephone Pioneers and the indefatigable Gigi Galassini founded the Telephone Pioneer Museum of New Mexico in 1997. An operator who worked her way up through the system, Galassini worked with the Pioneers and stockpiled artifacts. The group's Pioneer Room was a movable feast, appearing in multiple venues, but in 1996, the museum moved into this fully restored 1906 facility. Volunteers run it, and among its fascinating items is the switchboard operated during Pancho Villa's raid on Columbus in southern New Mexico.

Our Grocery Store

Albuquerque's large Italian community traces its roots back to the nineteenth century. Some men came alone to establish themselves and then sent for their families; others immigrated in groups. Several went into the grocery business. This store was built at Seventh and Tijeras in 1904 for Alessandro Matteucci. It opened in 1905. Upstairs was the family home. Note that the signs are printed in both English and Spanish, as most business was conducted in both languages. *Abarrotes* are groceries; a *carniceria* is a meat market. Across the street, the family had an apartment building. Matteucci operated the store until 1938. Some of the extended family ran the popular Paris Shoe Store, which sold fancy footware until recently.

After Alessandro Matteucci left in 1938, other grocers and meat markets, such as Hawkins, Kimmel, and Frank's, carried on. The store is adjacent to Immaculate Conception Church, which perhaps explains why Matteucci selected this location. For a time, this was where uniforms for students in all of Albuquerque's parochial schools were purchased. The original family home upstairs is divided into apartments, which are occupied. The building was remodeled to accommodate two businesses. Today, a design studio and an architectural firm occupy the first floor.

Albuquerque's first armory was at the intersection of Front (First) and Gold Avenue, a plain frame building. The Hotel Alvarado replaced it. The building was frequently used for balls and fund-raisers, and was the site of the first film shown in town. A new convention hall was built at Silver and Fifth in 1908, in time for Albuquerque to host the Sixteenth National Irrigation Congress. Later it was used as the National Guard Armory. The towers and crenellated battlements made it peculiar among other burgeoning buildings. It was used for conventions, sewing shows, boxing, wrestling, and live music performances. In 1955, a young Elvis Presley appeared here. According to master of ceremonies Bill Previtti, girls were screaming so loud that he couldn't introduce Elvis.

After the Civic Auditorium opened in 1956, the armory wasn't used as frequently. The New Mexico National Guard built a new facility. The building was converted to an ordinary-looking office building and was occupied by various businesses. The modified armory was razed in 1999. The new building is the Public Service Company of New Mexico's parking garage.

It is deliberately different and adds a touch of fancy to downtown. The front features brown and silver metal "waves," which pick up the river theme in the cityscape on its west side. It is an eye-catcher and it takes the viewer a moment to realize it's a garage.

This is the New Mexico Statehood Parade, passing by Fourth and Central. New Mexico was a territory for sixty-two years; it was not annexed because it was viewed as as rural, impoverished, uneducated, and backward. The Rosenwald Building (left) was Albuquerque's first department store and first fireproof building. McLellan's five-and-dime was on the first floor for decades. The Yrisarri Block (right) was built in 1909. It housed drugstores, a Hallmark shop, and Maisel's Indian Store. Upstairs were offices. The Yrisarri was unusual because it never housed a walkup hotel. The facade was painted and modernized to attract customers, but architecture, like fashion, is fickle.

McLellan's, like all five-and-dimes, eventually closed. Its landmark silver cantilevered aluminum awning came down. The gracious Rosenwald Building now has a Quizno's Subs downstairs and offices upstairs. It remains a magnificent edifice and is listed in the National Register of Historic Places. Nick Manole, the son of Greek parents who came to America empty-handed and battled impossible odds to achieve success, bought the Yrisarri Block and painstakingly restored the building to its Victorian grandeur. The Manoles run two restaurants in the building, Nick's and Fresh Choices. His mother works in the family business. The Rosenwald and Yrisarri buildings stand stalwart, just as they did when the Statehood Parade proudly passed by.

Albuquerque rented space on Second Street and Tijeras for city offices, in what may have been a house. No photos survive, and the exact location can't be determined from insurance maps. At one point, the owner sued the city for about seventy dollars in back rent. Disagreements over where to put the city hall, proposed designs, and costs continued for about a dozen years.

Finally, a parcel of land was selected cater-corner from city hall's second temporary site. The new building housed offices, as well as police and fire departments, pictured here around 1914. This facility, with a later addition for jailbirds, was utilized into the 1960s, when city hall was relocated to Fourth and Marquette.

In the 1970s, entire blocks of Victorian houses and buildings, including the old Strong Building that once housed a furniture store and funeral parlor, as well as the family home upstairs, were leveled. So were many commercial concerns, such as Mike London's Golden West Cocktail Lounge. Today, in their place, is First Plaza, or the Galeria, built by First National Bank. The Galeria is a great place to spend the afternoon. One can visit fine gift shops, browse art galleries, buy clothes, or get a driver's license renewed at the Department of Motor Vehicles.

The Occidental Life Insurance Building is one of Albuquerque's most fascinating structures. The architect, Henry C. Trost of El Paso, Texas, was employed to work on this miniature palace, strongly influenced by the Doge's Palace in Venice. Finished in 1917, the offices were set back beneath the cornices, making the south and east porches under the arcades nine feet deep. One of three fires on the night of April 24, 1933, devastated the roof and the interior. The nearby Fourth Ward School and the McCanna House also burned. Fortunately, the Occidental survived.

Local architect W. Miles Britelle Sr. redesigned the Occidental Life Building in 1934. Britelle re-created the roof to look even more like that of the Doge's Palace, and added ornate trim to the roofline. The office space was extended so that the porches under the arcades disappeared, although an illusion of depth was maintained. The exterior was repaired with glazed white terra-cotta tile, supplied by the original company, thus preserving its historical integrity.

In 1981, a two-story office building was built inside the original walls. From the exterior, it appears to have one story, surprising the visitor who steps inside. The building has recently been occupied by Tally Systems, a subdivision of Novell, the computer software and services provider. The Occidental is an unusual landmark—a Venetian palace in a Southwestern desert town.

MAISEL'S · INDIAN · TRADING · POST ·

MAISEL'S

MAISEL'S INDIAN TRADING POST — 510 W. Central Ave. — ALBUQUERQUE, NEW MEXICO

Maurice Maisel was an early entrepreneur who, from the beginning of his career, always said he wanted "the real thing." Maurice supervised Western Union telegram delivery boys, and those who worked for him remember him as a kind boss. Maisel bought a store on south First Street, across from the Hotel Alvarado and began a lifelong career in Native American arts. He and his wife lived above the store. The family business expanded and at one time or another, has had stores in Winrock Mall, the Yrisarri Building, and this one on west Central.

John Gaw Meem created today's building. Maurice said he did not want "the usual Indian thing." The result was this unique Pueblo Deco store, with recessed showcase windows and Native American murals on the facade. Noted artist Olive Rush designed the murals, and shared the painting process with Native American artists such as Harrison Begay, Pablita Velarde, Pop Chalee, and others whose names are now canon in Southwestern art. Maisel's staff created crafts in the downstairs workshop. Visitors enjoyed looking down and watching the process.

J.C. Penney opened in 1916 in the two-story Melini Building. J.C. Penney was one of, if not the first, national chain stores in the city. S.H. Kress (seen in the photograph opposite) opened in 1925, during the heyday of the five-and-dime. Albuquerque Gas and Electric (the second building from the left in this photograph) once had dozens of incandescent lights that lit up the night when the sun went down. The Queen Anne–style Garcia-Bliss Building (to the right of the Gas and Electric Building) appeared between 1903 and 1908, according to Sanborn Insurance maps. Upstairs was the Elgin Hotel, accessed by a long wooden walk-up staircase. Downstairs, over the years, was a tire vulcanizing center, a shoe store, and the Coney Island Café.

J.C. Penney opened a satellite store in the fashionable Northeast Heights area. The downtown store remained open, but as malls opened, J.C. Penney relocated. The downtown store closed in the 1970s. The Gizmo Store, which occupies the site today, sells work clothing. When the dime-store era ended,

Kress closed. The Gas and Electric Building has offices upstairs and a restaurant on the lower floor. All of the downtown walk-up hotels are gone now. Lindy's restaurant in the Garcia-Bliss Building maintains the tradition of old Coney Island and is a popular lunch spot, serving a 1950s menu.

The White Elephant Saloon originally stood on the corner of South Second and West Railroad (Central) Avenue. Built by New York transplant Joe Barnett, its bar could accommodate fifty men—and only men. No nice girl would be seen in a place like this. In the 1920s, Barnett demolished it and erected the Sunshine Theater. The saloon probably faltered when Prohibition was ratified and legal liquor sales were banned. The new theater was all the rage, and it's said that the mayor's wife, Carrie Tingley, held reserved seating and attended daily. The Sunshine premiered *Gone With the Wind* in 1939. The film was so long, patrons were advised to bring a lunch.

Suburban theaters and large multiplexes stole business from the downtown movie palaces. The Sunshine ceased showing films in the 1980s, but offices and business spaces continued to operate there. The stately building, designed by Henry C. Trost of the architectural firm Trost & Trost of El Paso, Texas, was added to the National Register of Historic Places in 1985. In the 1990s, it was remodeled to accommodate live performances, and on weekends is packed with young people while lively music and dancers spill into the streets.

Movies were considered to be for the lower classes until respectable ladies starting attending matinees projected on sheets in storefronts. When the economic potential of the cinema was understood, entrepreneurs erected picture palaces in imitation of European opera houses. Italian American Oreste Bachechi wanted to honor New Mexico's first citizens and create a cinematic castle for Albuquerque. Bachechi sent designer Carl Bolles around the state to gather design impressions. The KiMo is Pueblo Deco—Art Deco furnishings and heavy, stepped-back massing that imitates indigenous architecture. Inside were skulls with glowing eyes, Native American funeral canoes, air vents that looked like Navajo rugs, and a railing of wrought-iron birds. Isleta Pueblo's Pablo Abeita won $100 for giving it the name KiMo, which means "king of its kind." It opened in 1927 to much acclaim.

The KiMo offered movies and live performances. Young Vivian Vance, Lucille Ball's sidekick Ethel, acted, sang, and danced here. Road shows, burlesques, reviews, and films kept the KiMo vibrant for decades. When downtown theaters failed, the KiMo closed. It was almost lost but for a handful of persevering preservationists. The city purchased it, and it is now restored, with meticulously re-created historic elements. The theater is a venue for all manner of live events. Performers maintain a shrine to a little boy who was killed in 1951 when a boiler exploded—as long as Bobby is appeased, performances go off without incident. The KiMo is a monument to Oreste Bachechi, Native American design, and Albuquerque's past.

Charles Wright came to Albuquerque from Kansas. He worked with the Fred Harvey Company's Indian stores. In 1907 he and his family returned to Albuquerque and in 1917 erected Wright's Indian Trading Post & Curios at Fourth and Gold. The fabulous building, with ladders, vigas (roof beams), *hornos* (adobe ovens), and other accoutrements, invoked Pueblo architecture.

Once the Santa Fe Railway called attention to Native American arts, imitation rings and necklaces were available at five-and-dimes and curio shops. Vendors such as Wright, the Maisel family, and the White Eagle Trading Post offered jewelry that wouldn't turn one's skin green. A block from Route 66, Wright's was a tremendous tourist attraction.

Wright died in 1938, but his wife, Kathryn, kept the business open until she sold it in the 1950s to the Chernoff family, a French-Russian couple, now deceased, who loved Native American creations. Their gallery maintains original integrity, although Wright's Indian Art is now located uptown.

The old trading post was razed to make room for a second, taller skyscraper, the Bank of New Mexico Building, east of the Simms Tower. The building now bears the name New Mexico Bank & Trust. This photograph shows the view from east of the original Wright's.

The Angus A. Grant Building was erected on the northwest corner of Third Street and Railroad (Central) in 1883. Grant was a Canadian railroad man, after whom the town of Grants, New Mexico, is named. The Charles Ilfeld Company, which dealt in dry goods, occupied the first floor. The Grant Opera House and a banquet room were upstairs. Although it sounds grand, and some famous stars twinkled on its stage, patrons sat on hard wooden benches. A spectacular fire destroyed the building in 1898. The Golden Rule Dry Goods occupied the rebuilt structure, but the opera house was never reconstructed, nor was the landmark pointed cupola. Mr. Giomi, a prominent member of Albuquerque's Italian-American community, bought the building prior to 1931 and remodeled it at a cost of $5,000.

Kistler Collister, a popular high-end women's clothing store, occupied this building for several decades. For a time, the Albuquerque Business College taught typing and filing classes upstairs. In the 1950s, Kistler Collister remodeled the store with a dramatic flair, covering most of the windows and giving it a more streamlined modern look. When Kistler Collister followed other downtown merchants to Northeast Heights, the American Bank of Commerce and the Quinn Company occupied the building. It has had several occupants since then. Whatever was left of the venerable old walls was recently removed, and this fanciful new place was created in its stead, adding a little spice to the corner.

The Art Deco Skinner Building was erected in 1931 as a grocery store. It was the first in A. J. Skinner's chain. Food stores were important during the tentative days of refrigeration, and many women shopped for fresh meat and produce daily. Because people lived in or near downtown, there were many mom-and-pop corner stores, along with larger stores such as Skinner's. After supermarkets began to appear and Albuquerque started inching toward the east side, many of these markets declined. The building housed a Pepsi-Cola Company office and various other concerns over the years. The Skinner family sold the building in 1970, and the city bought the place in 1977. It was sold to the current owner with the proviso that the facades be preserved.

The Skinner Building is now home to Villa di Capo, an Italian restaurant. The Art Deco ornamentation—zigzags, chevrons, and other shapes—are still extant. It is a valuable architectural form in a city that has little of the Art Deco genre. The owner wanted to add an outside terrace when downtown dining at night became popular. Historic preservationists objected, citing the previous agreement with the city and expressing concern that the addition would conceal elegant elements and alter a historic treasure. Hearings and debates ensued, but the owner prevailed and Villa di Capo now has its balcony addition. As the photo shows, the Art Deco elements are still preserved and somewhat visible.

The Hotel Franciscan was built by public subscription in 1923, as tourism was increasing and Albuquerque felt it needed another luxury hotel. It soon rivaled the Hotel Alvarado. The large building incorporated Pueblo architecture and was an impressive sight at the corner of Central Avenue and Sixth Street. It was a tourist attraction in itself. Inside were dark tile floors and rich, Spanish-themed furniture. The hotel rapidly became another social center for the town, hosting dances, balls, meals, and an annual New Year's Eve bash. When a mah-jongg craze swept the nation, ladies met in the hotel to play. One bridge club maintained a suite of rooms there for weekly play, which started at precisely 12:01 p.m.

Railroad travel lost its cachet as aviation and the automobile took its place. Like the Alvarado and Hilton, the Franciscan lost money to the motels that sprang up right beside the highways. People preferred to stay in the less-expensive places and enjoyed the quick access to their cars. Fewer people came to shop and have lunch as residents flocked to suburban shopping malls. Driving downtown became more problematic, as Route 66 ran right down Central Avenue and the growing volume of traffic included increasingly larger trucks. Gridlock prevailed. When the interstate highways were completed, downtown was bypassed. In 1972, the Hotel Franciscan was demolished. Whether it was architecturally sound or not is still a subject likely to arouse debate, but rumor says it would not yield to the wrecking ball and had to be dynamited.

The Atchison, Topeka, and Santa Fe Railway was established in Albuquerque in 1880 and its base grew until its facilities went from First and Central to five miles out into the country, where a tie-treating plant operated. Initially the silver tracks cut the old Hispanic plaza of Barelas in half, severing it from the common grazing lands by the sand hills. Not everyone profited from the arrival of the railroad. But as rural farms around New Mexico failed from poverty, drought, unpaid taxes, and disasters, people moved into Albuquerque and Barelas became the hub of the railroad-working world. Between a third and a half of the town's working men received their paycheck from the railroad. These men are checking out, but in a few hours, the big whistle will punctuate their day—telling them when to arise, eat lunch, and go home after a ten- or twelve-hour shift.

Multiple factors led to the railroad's decline. This was the largest shop in the Southwest, running 24-7, keeping the Santa Fe's locomotives in service. But the railroad itself began dieselization, and, in a sense, cut its own throat. Diesel engines require less maintenance, and so as they began to replace locomotives, the shops slowed down. People traveled less on trains and more often flew or drove themselves. The shops rallied during World War II as trains transported troops from coast to coast. Young matrons and maidens of the community spent time serving lunches "and a smile" to boys who never came home. Peace ended the temporary revival, and gradually the great staff dropped to skeleton crews until there was no more work.

A locomotive tender is backed out of a workshop of the Atchison, Topeka, and Santa Fe Railway shops in 1943, headed for the transfer turntable. The shops were constantly updated and replaced. These 1921 buildings replaced the early workshops. A new roundhouse appeared, and it seemed as though the railroad would roll on forever. These enormous buildings resembled cathedrals, with their multicolored windowpanes. Industrial historians have compared the efficient design of the complex to the Ford Motor Company's glass plant of 1922. In addition to the boiler shop and machine shop, there was a blacksmiths' shop, flue shop, and sheet metal shed. If the whistle blew at an off time, everyone knew that someone had suffered an accident.

Today the railroad shops are abandoned. The buildings are under lock and key to prevent vandalism and accidents. However, tours are conducted for the curious and for educational purposes. The Wheels Museum, incorporated in 1997, has set out to save the shops and works incessantly to acquire the property and save it from demolition. The organization seeks to establish a transportation museum. One day it may be possible to see old locomotives, motorcycles, cars, bicycles, and every form of transportation here. However, developers are still keen to acquire the site and remove the old sheds. Though plans to convert it to a film studio have fallen through, further light industrial use of the site has been considered.

With the dawn of the railroad, a previously subsistent, hand-to-mouth economy suddenly began to thrive. A wool scouring plant, wool mill, flour mill, warehouses, and mercantile companies soon filled the railroad corridor. This Southwestern Brewery and Ice Company structure was built in 1898, after operating in smaller buildings. It is a five-story brick stock house. The critical ice needed to keep food cold was manufactured along with Glorieta beer—produced for Albuquerque's many saloons, as the sign announces in huge letters: "Home of Glorieta Beer." According to historian Marc Simmons, the company brewed 30,000 barrels of the brew yearly, and froze forty-five tons of ice every day. The brewery was added to the National Register of Historic Places in 1978. Glorieta beer bottles and caps still sometimes surface around town.

After refrigerators were perfected, the iceman in his horse-drawn wagon or motorized truck was no longer needed. The Southwestern Brewery and Ice Company was still making ice as late as the 1970s, according to Susan Dewitt's 1978 survey of extant historic places. All operations have now ceased, and the forlorn building sits empty alongside the tracks, though it still faintly proclaims to be the home of Glorieta beer. In the late 1990s a fire razed some of the surrounding smaller structures. Luckily, the main plant was saved; however, its future use is uncertain.

In the 1900s, "good roads" groups began to form, along with concern that historic national trails were not being adequately marked and would disappear. The Daughters of the American Revolution and the National Old Trails Road Association joined to promote the new roads and save the old. They designed a monument, a pioneer mother carrying a baby in one arm and a rifle in the other, with a small child clinging to her skirts. The statue is on a six-foot base and stands ten feet tall. Twelve statues were made, and trail towns were selected to receive them. New Mexico's went to Santa Fe but was rejected by its art community. Albuquerque took the monument instead. She was dedicated at McClellan Park with much pomp in 1928.

MADONNA OF THE TRAIL

N·S·D·A·R· MEMORIAL
TO THE
PIONEER MOTHERS
OF THE
COVERED WAGON DAYS

A time capsule was deposited in the Madonna's base in 1928, containing newspaper clippings, a list of contributor names, and contest manuscripts submitted for the base's inscriptions. In 1978, the DAR searched for the capsule and even had the base X-rayed, but it was not recovered. Despite community concern over losing a green space, McClellan Park was designated as the site for a new federal courthouse in the 1990s. The DAR and other concerned parties made certain that the Madonna was refurbished and remained near her original site. When they dismantled her base, the time capsule was found and taken to the Albuquerque Museum. It had fallen below the base and the contents, for the most part, were stuck together and unreadable, but at least the mystery had finally been solved.

Newly arrived Protestant families wanted education for their children. In 1879, Colorado College, an institution supporting private schools in the west, established the Albuquerque Academy (not today's Academy) just outside the plaza. In 1882 it moved to New Town. The academy needed its own building. Money was raised, and in 1890 this three-story brick-and-stone beauty was erected at Railroad (Central) and Edith. Arno Huning, son of the neighborhood's developer, Franz Huning, was one of the students. The city rented Perkins Hall for its new Albuquerque High School. This building, now gone, remains critical to local history because public education in New Town (now Albuquerque) started here.

The first public library was in the Commercial Club, created by prominent local women who organized the Library Ball. Seeing their efforts to better the community, businesses made healthy donations to the cause. In 1900, Joshua and Sarah Raynolds gave Perkins Hall to the city to be used as a library. Books soon filled the second floor. There were two small fires in 1923. In 1924 the city demolished Perkins Hall, making way for a larger building to accommodate the town's growth. A beautifully designed Spanish Pueblo–style building replaced Perkins Hall. It was the main library until a large branch was built downtown. Today it houses special collections and genealogical materials. It is well worth a visit to see the exquisite interior.

Albuquerque High held classes in a little house on South Edith, and in Perkins Hall. In 1900, the Central School was built at Third and Lead for junior high and high school students. In 1914, this Collegiate-Gothic building opened at Broadway and Central and upper classes moved in. Critics said it was too big—the town's students would never need that much space. Before too long, more buildings were added. Most of the older generation of Albuquerque graduated here, as it was the only public high school until Highland High School opened in 1949. Athletic competitions were held with the Indian School, the Menaul School, St. Mary's, and the university. The campus closed in 1974 when a new Albuquerque High opened in Martineztown.

Albuquerque High's old buildings sat vacant for many years and gradually fell into disrepair. Broken windows and high fences eventually replaced the once-busy campus. Alumni grieved while several different preservation schemes came and went. Some believed the solution was to clear the land and start anew. In 1998, Paradigm and Company started rebuilding despite community skepticism. Now the buildings are all but filled by loft apartments, family homes, and amenities. Growth continues, with other facilities in the planning or building phases. Residents seem pleased to be able to walk to work, just as downtown dwellers did when Albuquerque was small.

Carothers and Fuller was in the heart of Huning's Highland, Albuquerque's first subdivision. Wealthy Franz Huning purchased land and plotted the neighborhood eight months after the railroad hit town in 1880. Railroad employees, merchants, lawyers, doctors, and other professionals moved in. The houses ranged from mansions to cottages, although almost all reflected the Victorian architecture that was popular at the time. At first, primitive conditions ruled, with windmills, outhouses, vegetable gardens, and chickens. With each amenity that became available, the neighborhood became more pleasant. But as Albuquerque moved east, the business corridor along Central changed. This building appeared in the late 1930s, no doubt in response to the rerouting of Route 66 down Central. Carothers and Fuller offered one-stop service, selling tires and batteries.

People left their homes downtown and in Huning's Highland to head for the hills. After World War II, when Northeast Heights offered rows of tract homes, the mansions of the Highlands were abandoned. Some were divided into apartments. The neighborhood became a low-rent, high-crime district. When I-25 was constructed, stately manors were razed to make room for motels and eateries. In the 1970s, as historic preservation gained momentum, "urban pioneers" returned. Today, the Huning's Highland Neighborhood Association diligently ousts criminals and fights to maintain historic integrity and a safe neighborhood. This building held many car services, including Das Autohaus in the mid-1980s. The Standard Diner reflects the revitalization of the area. The area is called East Downtown Huning's Highland.

In 1902, the Sisters of Charity opened the impressive St. Joseph Sanatorium, Albuquerque's first tuberculosis hospital. Many ancillary services followed, and medicine began to underpin the local economy. Tuberculosis was grist for dramas such as *Camille* and operas like *La Traviata,* and was commonly known as consumption because the pale, thin victims wasted away. There was no cure, only care—altitude, dry air, and hope, all of which Albuquerque and New Mexico had in abundance. The city's promoters touted the "salubrious" climate and promised recovery, knowing patients would bring families, doctors, and money, even though the city was struggling to keep pace with the influx of patients.

St. Joseph Sanatorium expanded until it filled up several blocks from what is now I-25 west to Edith Boulevard. It offered a wide range of services, building a regular hospital in the 1920s. After the discovery of antibiotics during the 1940s, tuberculosis was defeated and the establishment changed its role to a full-service medical facility. Some people who came to "chase the cure" recovered and stayed on to contribute to New Mexico. Because there are no statistics, it is unclear if palliative and sometimes peculiar treatments helped, or if some folks just got well. St. Joseph Hospital served the community for one hundred years before it was sold and is now part of the Lovelace Sandia Health System.

In 1906, Dr. Charles Lukens, pastor of a Roswell, New Mexico, church, organized the New Mexico and Arizona Children's Home Society, and he and his family moved into this house. By 1910, as census records show, several orphaned and sick children resided in this home. The square addition was very likely a dormitory. Dr. Lukens specialized in helping children recuperate from birth defect surgeries, and in placing orphans in "childless homes." However, not all came to him by this route. One newborn addition to his household was found on the seat of a passenger train at the depot.

Dr. Lukens's house stood until the late 1950s and it can often be seen in photographs of the Civic Auditorium, which was built (and later destroyed) nearby. Lukens moved into the new orphanage across the street (see page 119) in 1921. In 1944, he was debilitated by illness. He died in 1948. Apparently, St. Joseph Hospital to the west razed the building. Many other classy homes on this block and the next fell to the freeway, which is just east of the property. The Heart Hospital of New Mexico can be seen through the trees. A facility that caters just to hearts seems to be an appropriate symbol for a man whose own heart was so big.

This is the brand-new Children's Home and Hospital that Dr. Charles Lukens built in 1921 with generous help from the community. We know that infants were cared for, as the local Masons affectionately referred to the facility as the "Temple of Babies' Smiles." The impressive structure had twenty rooms, a gigantic underground garage, marvelously modern medical equipment, and sleeping porches. Sleeping outside for robust health was a practice adopted for tuberculosis patients and one that spread to the general public. There was an on-site school, and many local luminaries served on the executive board.

Dr. Lukens vacated his orphanage in 1944 and returned to his home across the street. City directories suggest that some children continued to reside with him. He sold the building to St. Joseph Hospital for use as the Regina School of Nursing, overseen by the Sisters of Charity. Many local nurses graduated from this institute. The site is now occupied by Eye Associates of New Mexico. The pleasant sleeping porches have been converted to offices and a waiting room. Some modifications have been made, but Regina Hall retains historic integrity. Employees say that if you are there alone at night, you frequently hear the soft footsteps of little feet down the corridors, and the whispers and giggles of children.

Health-seekers poured into Albuquerque, encouraged by boosters. Although St. Joseph opened in 1902, there were more patients than places. Dr. Hugh Cooper came in 1903 to heal his tuberculosis. In 1908 he started the Presbyterian Sanatorium in Henry Brockmeier's cottage. Dr. Cooper was joined by Marion Kellogg van Devanter, who brought her ailing husband, Jimmy. He died, but "Mrs. Van" stayed. When Dr. Cooper passed in 1934,

Mrs. Van kept the "San" going, visited patients daily, and assisted every administrator until her death in the 1980s. She raised funds so everyone could receive treatment. This picture shows the main building (left), Brockmeier's house (right), and tent cottages in between. Presbyterian provided large meals; hours in the sun, called "heliotherapy"; outdoor sleeping; surgery; and every treatment available.

After antibiotics trampled tuberculosis, Presbyterian had a few rough moments and its future was in doubt. The board and Mrs. Van decided to convert the facility to a full-service hospital. The old buildings were torn down in the 1960s to make room for the towers pictured here. Growth never slowed, and by the 1980s Presbyterian had an ambulance service, a statewide hospital network, a satellite hospital (Anna Kaseman) in the heights, and all the latest medical equipment. This complex now has multiple buildings, filled with care ranging from delivering babies to complex surgeries. In 2008, Presbyterian will celebrate its hundredth birthday. Presbyterian is New Mexico's only home-owned nonprofit hospital. This photograph features the west side of the buildings, as the front was temporarily obscured by construction.

This photo looks west on Central Avenue in 1943. Immediately to the right of the billboard is the Atchison, Topeka, and Santa Fe Railway Hospital, opened primarily as a tuberculosis sanatorium for railroad workers in 1926. This building replaced the old railroad hospital on South Broadway. After tuberculosis came under control, the hospital continued to care for railroad men. South Oak Street is in the foreground, still an ordinary cross street on the west side of Presbyterian Sanatorium. The First National Bank building is just visible in the distance to the right of Central Avenue.

Today, the same shot looking west on Central is barely recognizable. All of the houses are gone, even the few that were added on storefronts and operated home businesses. The Santa Fe Railway's Memorial Hospital buildings still stand, but now serve as a psychiatric facility. Southeast Oak Street is a fast one-way frontage road sandwiched between I-25 and Presbyterian Hospital. The freeway now occupies all of the vacant land once seen between Oak and the railroad hospital. Although First National Bank survives, two new skyscrapers with their pyramid-shaped roofs overshadow it.

The University of New Mexico was founded in 1889 but had no home of its own. Classes met in Perkins Hall at Edith and Railroad Avenue (Central). They moved to University Hall, later renamed Hodgin Hall after distinguished professor and administrator Charles Hodgin. This photo shows the west side of the building. Everything—offices, classrooms, and other services—was in this rather Gothic-looking Richardsonian Romanesque building. The sandy road leading up to University Hall was all but impassable. With the advent of automobiles, drivers were at times embarrassed when their little buzz wagons had to be pulled out by actual horsepower. A second building, Hadley Hall, erected a few years later, housed laboratories, including ones for domestic sciences. Hadley Hall later burned to the ground.

William George Tight became president of UNM in 1901. He fell in love with the Pueblo Indian culture surrounding Albuquerque and decided that the empty campus should be filled with buildings that looked like New Mexico and not like Ohio, from whence he came. Tight added two buildings—Kwataka and Hokona halls—dormitories for men and women. He built a kiva, a building that resembled a Native American ceremonial structure, which was used by a fraternity, and then he remodeled Hodgin Hall. This is the east side of Hodgin Hall today. The west view is obscured by trees. The roof was flattened, the walls covered with adobe-colored stucco. It was "puebloized." Fierce criticism ensued and Tight lost his appointment. Ironically, what he began continued, and now UNM's unique architecture is a source of pride.

A house for the president of UNM was built in the 1930s, sitting on empty land at Yale and Las Lomas. It was constructed during the Great Depression, but funds had already been appropriated. The Spanish Pueblo Revival–style dwelling fit right in with the other regional buildings—by then, widely accepted as UNM's special signature. The house was adequate at the time, but as the years passed, larger homes with more features became a standard. Van Dorn Hooker, the university's architect, remodeled the kitchen and created a family room for William Davis. Apparently a plan was advanced that excluded the dwelling but, fortunately, it was never effected and the house is now included in the National Register of Historic Places.

UNM presidents usually lived in the house. During some tenures, additions were made—for example, another bathroom was added to the private living quarters. Some presidents elected to remain in their local homes and avoid relocating their children to new schools. When Richard Peck became head of the university, the house was remodeled and it was renamed University House and became available for meetings and events. Its most notorious occupation was in 1969, when one of a series of campus unrests erupted, as they did all over the country. Following a speech by Jane Fonda, about 300 students jammed into the courtyard and some climbed onto the roof, shouting demands down the chimney. Several were arrested. President Ferrel Heady, who had chosen to live in the house, wisely decided to avoid a confrontation and stayed inside.

The University of New Mexico's first "library" was a room in Hodgin Hall. At one time, it also served as the campus post office. Although faculty and administrators recognized that books were critical to learning, there was never quite enough money to buy them. When Hadley Hall, the science building, burned down, a replacement building and other pressing needs had to be met. Finally, in 1926, UNM opened its first real library, east of Hodgin Hall. The entire collection was hand-carried to the new facility. The library was supposed to last for many years, but within a decade it was deemed too small.

University architect John Gaw Meem designed a replacement library. With pomp and circumstance, the small library's collections were once again moved in 1938, into the library named after UNM's president and financed with WPA funds. James Zimmerman proudly led the parade; Mrs. Zimmerman carried the first book; the marching band played; and students, faculty, and staff followed. This time, the considerably larger collection was transported by trucks. During both moves, both libraries stayed open and services were never interrupted. John Gaw Meem's design left room for growth. Several new additions have been made without compromising the building's original beauty. The Meem portion of the building is used by the Center for Southwest Research and houses rare book and manuscript collections.

This little triangular slab of land was created by the intersection of three "new" streets: Girard, Central, and Monte Vista. In around 1929, C. M. Dyer built Albuquerque's first drive-in, the Triangle. It was open 24-7, had carhops, and served barbecue, among other delicacies. In 1935 Dyer moved his establishment across the street and it became the Triangle Bar. Its neon sign, a three-sided equilateral, could be seen around the Monte Vista neighborhood at night. A new eatery for cars occupied this site until the 1990s, when one of the last vestiges of full-service motoring was razed.

Albuquerque had four of these small, self-contained trailer diners. This one, the Little House Diner, was downtown for years and was a lively place for folks who worked in the area. These were Valentine Diners, made in Kansas. They had four to eight seats, and two people could operate them. The diner is a legacy of the old horse-drawn "lunch wagons" that brought dinner to night workers in large cities. Joe and Della Lucero owned this one until the 1990s, when they donated it to the Albuquerque Museum. The museum and the city placed the diner on the Triangle, where it now serves as a police substation.

This house was built in 1928 at the corner of Dartmouth and Girard Place Northeast. William Leverett Sr. came to Albuquerque in 1915 to treat his tuberculosis. He recovered, and in 1926 began building the Monte Vista subdivision. The house is Spanish Pueblo Revival and is larger than it looks. Inside, it is reminiscent of an old hacienda, dark, quiet, and cool. There is a full basement, which at one time contained laundry facilities and a huge natural gas heater. Mrs. Leverett Sr. lived here until the 1950s. William Leverett Jr. carried on the family business. Some parts of this land were owned by UNM while homesteaders occupied others. Across the street, not visible in the photo, is Monte Vista Elementary, built on the site of J. F. Sulzer's ranch.

The Leverett House is a historic landmark. The little houses to the north mark the beginnings of the Monte Vista neighborhood, which soon contained many homes, two churches, the school, and a burgeoning business district. This land is irregular, and the streets, which are named after colleges, twist, curve, and climb up and down the small hills. This forces traffic to slow down and also allows water from sudden downpours to flow down to Campus Boulevard. Sweeps of water once carried away many small toys and shoes, to the delight of neighborhood kids. The street alignment created several triangular patches of land, which now hold buildings and are extremely unique. This area is now considered part of the Nob Hill District.

There's a saying in Albuquerque: If you want to know where the city's headed, watch car dealers. In 1939, Ralph Jones built a service station, auto dealership, and repair shop at 3222 Central Avenue Southeast, in the Nob Hill area. It is Streamline Moderne, with curved walls and a decorative tower. Inside is yellow "penitentiary brick," made by prison inmates. Jones was a real Route 66 booster. His daughter recalls that during the Depression, he donated time helping passing "Okies" repair sick vehicles. The World War II years were slow, with tires and gas rationed. Sales increased after the war when people, after waiting four years, were ready for a brand-new car. Jones moved again in 1957, predicting growth toward Lomas and San Mateo.

After Ralph Jones relocated, the building hosted many concerns, including a Goodwill outlet, a moped shop, and various others. In 1999, Janice and Dennis Bonfantine of Kelly's Brewery bought the store. The Nob Hill neighborhood wanted to turn the buildings into a new community center, so there were some legal wrangles. Now it is Kelly's Brew Pub. They've installed a faux Texaco sign and some old gasoline pumps. The place goes neon after dark, and there's always a crowd sitting outside enjoying the old Route 66 atmosphere and the food and drink. The Jones family gathered for a reunion and was honored by the Bonfantines at a private opening. This renovation is a wonderful example of adaptive reuse.

AZTEC COURT — ALBUQUERQUE, NEW MEXICO

ON U. S. HIGHWAY 66

3821 EAST CENTRAL AVENUE

The Aztec Court motel on East Central was built out on the mesa in 1931, preceding the realignment of Route 66 by six years. Either the owner had exceptional foresight or knew something that nobody else did. The Aztec was a real court, not an open-air camp that offered gas and perhaps a hose to wash your hands or drink from. It had tourist appeal, with little nooks to park the precious car, and a quasi Spanish-Indian look with the second story over the office. It went through a few changes, beginning as the Aztec Auto Court, becoming the Aztec Lodge, and is now the Aztec Motel.

The Aztec is a priceless jewel because it is one of the few original Route 66 motels standing. As business declined with the opening of the interstate, many motels became crime centers and have since been razed. The Aztec has also become a monument to folk art and a sort of outdoor museum. Its exterior is covered with bric-a-brac, gewgaws, angels, velvet, windmills, bottles, flowers—drivers have constant near-misses, trying to gawk and drive at the same time. Owner Mohamed Natha knows he has a treasure and intends to keep it. The Aztec is the oldest motel still operating on Route 66.

The rise of automobile tourism led roadside merchants to ask the question "If people are whizzing by at thirty miles per hour, will they see our sign?" This anxiety underpinned a new style of architecture—in which form really follows function. If they made the buildings symbolic of their contents, people would come. This style is called mimetic architecture. This restaurant is shaped like a sombrero—anyone could see that Mexican food was served inside. The first El Sombrero restaurant was on South Yale, and its round shape has been incorporated into another restaurant, the Quarters.

Roadside eateries such as El Sombrero and others, from Chicago to Los Angeles, were bypassed when large, controlled-access interstates appeared, driven by Dwight D. Eisenhower's passion for the German autobahn. The president believed that national security would best be served by long, fast stretches of highway for rapid movement. Slowly, the little independent places lost out to bigger chain stores just off the ramp. Albuquerque National Bank bought the land under the big hat, and soon a branch bank and parking lot filled the space. The age of drive-ins was yielding to the age of sit-down coffee shops with fake red leather booths, one of which soon appeared across the street.

The Iceberg is another example of mimetic architecture. Who wouldn't think of ice cream when this place appeared on the horizon? The Iceberg was located just east of the Triangle, near the University of New Mexico. On opening day everyone received a free cone. It had a jukebox, and sometimes local bands such as Bernie May's Collegians provided live jive and kids tripped the light fantastic. Originally it had just one "berg" but another was added later. It predated the realignment of Route 66 and catered mostly to students. Once the realignment of Route 66 was completed, in 1937, this must have looked like a desert mirage to people approaching from the east—something up ahead that could sink the *Titanic*.

People moved close to the university and soon stores, restaurants, service stations, and other necessities followed. The Lobo, an uptown movie house, opened to huge crowds in 1939 on the Iceberg's location. The Iceberg floated east to a new spot, out on the far edge of town. It resettled near what is now San Mateo. A second berg was added and the Iceberg offered auto and human refreshment. In 1953, an oil company leased the property and the Iceberg trekked north to Bernalillo, where it stood until it was demolished in the 1960s. This area, once the edge of nowhere, is now one of the busiest in town. So many businesses have occupied the site that it's difficult to know exactly where the old berg sat.

In 1910, Clyde Tingley accompanied his tubercular fiancée, Carrie Wooster, to the Southwest. They married, settled in Albuquerque, and Clyde became a politician. After Carrie healed, she spent her days visiting the sick and helping children. Clyde served as ward alderman and city commissioner, and served two terms as governor of New Mexico, after which he was elected chairman of the city commission, a position later known as mayor of Albuquerque. The patrician Franklin Delano Roosevelt took great pleasure in the feisty New Mexican. Because of this, and the efforts of Senator Dennis Chavez and others, the state received generous amounts of New Deal money. Tingley, working with Middle Rio Grande Conversancy funds and reclamation projects, supervised creation of a desert water park.

Tingley Beach, also called Conservancy Beach and, later, Ernie Pyle Beach in memory of Albuquerque's fallen war correspondent, had swimming and boating facilities. People claim the hamburgers were the best in town. These were the polio decades, when nobody knew what caused the devastating disease. Parents lived in fear as children fell victim, in this age of the iron lung and the March of Dimes. In 1937, New Mexico opened the Carrie

Tingley Hospital for Crippled Children in Hot Springs (now known as Truth or Consequences). Public swimming pools were suspect. When bacteria appeared in the beach's water, the park was closed and its structures demolished. It has recently been reopened as a fishing park, with a station for a narrow-gauge railroad that loops around recreational facilities.

INDEX

Abeita, Pablo 90
Acoma Pueblo 5
Albright, Claude 47
Albright, Franc 52
Albright, George 52
Albuquerque Convention Center 39
Albuquerque Country Club 23
Albuquerque High School 108, 110–111
Albuquerque Historical Society 11
Albuquerque Museum 11, 18, 107, 131
Albuquerque Museum Foundation 17
Albuquerque National Bank 54, 56–57, 138–139
Albuquerque Public Library 108–109
Albuquerque Regional Medical Center 114–115
Albuquerque Street Railroad 54
Alvarado, Hernando de 5
Alvarado Transportation Center 39, 71
American Legion 67
Ancestral Pueblo 5
Angus A. Grant Building 94
Apache Canyon 12
Armijo, Ambrosio 16
Armijo, Manuel 12
Armijo, Mariano 44
Armijo House 44–45, 46
Armijo School 26–27
Armijo Store and House 16–17
Armory 76–77
Atchison, Topeka, and Santa Fe Railway 38, 71, 100, 102
Atchison, Topeka, and Santa Fe Railway Hospital 122–123
Atrisco 26
Aztec Court Motel 136–137
Bachechi, Oreste 90
Bandstand 14–15
Barelas Bridges 28–29
Barnett, Joe 88
Bataan Methodist Memorial Hospital 64
Benevolent Order of Elks 47
Bernalillo 24
Bernalillo County 26, 27
Blueher, Herman 18
Blueher House 18–19
Blueher's Pond 18
Bolles, Carl 90
Bonfantine, Dennis 135
Bonfantine, Janice 135
Böttger, Charles 13
Böttger Mansion 12–13
Bridge Street 29
Britelle, W. Miles 83
Brockmeier, Henry 120
Bryant, General N. 52
Bryant Company Delivery Service 52
Camp Stoney 63
Campus Boulevard 133
Carleton, James 14
Carl's Jr. 140–141
Carothers and Fuller Service Station 112–113
Carrie Tingley Hospital for Crippled Children 143
Castle Huning 21, 22–23
Central Avenue 39, 98, 99, 100, 122–123, 130, 134
César Chávez Boulevard 29
Chaco Canyon 5
Champion Grocery 74–75
Chavez, Dennis 142

City Hall 80–81
Civic Auditorium 77, 117
Coal Avenue Viaduct 60
Collister, Kistler 95
Colorado College 108
Colorado Telephone Building 72–73
Colter, Mary 70
Commercial Club 68–69, 109
Coney Island Café 86, 87
Congregation Albert 66, 67
Cooper, Hugh 120
Coronado, Francisco Vásquez de 5
Cromwell, Oliver 54
Cromwell Block 54–55
Davis, William 126
Deluxe Auto Camp 30–31
Dennis Chavez Federal Building 46–47
Devanter, Marion Kellogg van 120, 121
Dewitt, Susan 105
Dyer, C. M. 130
East Convention Center 60–61
East Downtown Huning's Highland 113
Edith Boulevard 35, 115, 124
El Camino Real 29
Elgin Hotel 86
Elks Lodge 47
El Sombrero 138–139
Exchange Hotel 62
Fergusson, Erna 21
Fergusson, Harvey 21
Fifth Avenue 46
Fire Station 60–61
First and Central 40–41
First National Bank 48–49, 81, 122, 123
First Plaza Galeria 80–81
First Street 55, 84, 100
First United Methodist Church 64–65
Fonda, Jane 127
Fourth Street 62, 68, 80
Fourth Ward School 82
French's Mortuary 69
Fresh Choices 79
Front Street 40, 50, 76
Gabor, Zsa Zsa 59
Galassini, Gigi 73
Galeria 49
Garcia-Bliss Bulding 86–87
Gas and Electric Building 86–87
Gasparri, Father 8
Gatewood Road 27
Giomi Building 94–95
Girard Place 132
Gizmo Store 87
Gold Avenue 46, 50–51, 52–53, 54, 68, 76
Golden West Cocktail Lounge 81
Gold Street Caffè 53
Gold Street Lofts 51
Grant Opera House 50
Greater Albuquerque Chamber of Commerce 54–55
Greyhound station 71
Grunsfeld family 66
Guardhouse 14–15
Hacienda de Doña Luisa de Trujillo 20
Hadley Hall 124, 128
Harwood, Mrs. Thomas 64
Heady, Ferrel 127
Heart Hospital of New Mexico 116–117
Highland High School 110
Highland Hotel 42–43

Highway 85 29
Hilton, Conrad 59
Hilton Hotel 59
Hodgin Hall 124–125, 128
Hokona Hall 125
Hooker, Van Dorn 126
Hope's European Hotel 40
Hotel Alvarado 5, 36, 39, 42, 70–71, 76, 84
Hotel Franciscan 98–99
Hudson Hotel 42–43
Huning, Arno 23, 108
Huning, Clara 10, 21
Huning, Ernestine 20, 23
Huning, Franz 10, 20, 21, 22, 23, 112
Iceberg Café 140–141
Immaculate Conception Church 75
Indian Building 5
Isleta Boulevard 29
J.C. Penney building 86–87
Jones, Ralph 134
Jones Motor Company 134–135
Kaseman, George 56
Keleher, William 58
Kelly's Brew Pub 134–135
KiMo Theatre 90–91
Kiva Auditorium 61
Knights of Pythias Hall 50, 66
Kress building 86–87
Kwataka Hall 125
La Fonda del Bosque Restaurant 31
La Glorieta 20–21
La Hacienda Restaurant 18–19
La Placita Restaurant 16–17
La Posada 58–59
Leverett, William, Jr., 132
Leverett, William, Sr., 132
Leverett House 132–133
Little House Diner 131
Lobo 141
Lomas 134
London, Mike 81
Los Griegos Plaza 32–33
Los Lunas 29
Loyola Hall 9
Lucero, Della 131
Lucero, Joe 131
Lukens, Charles 116, 117, 118, 119
Lukens House 116–117
Madonna of the Trail 106–107
Main Street 14
Maisel, Maurice 84
Maisel's Indian Store 78, 84–85
Make-a-Wish Foundation 57
Mandell and Dreyfus 45
Manole, Nick 79
Manuel Armijo House 12–13
Manzano Day School 21
Martín, Don Manuel 34
Martineztown 34–35, 36, 37, 110
Matteucci, Alessandro 74, 75
McCanna House 82
McClennan Park 106, 107
McLellan's five-and-dime 78, 79
Meem, John Gaw 63, 85, 129
Melini Building 86
Meylett, Colonel 46
Monte Vista Elementary 132
Montoya, Atanacio 26
Mother Road 5
Napoleone family 30
Natha, Mohamed 137

National Hispanic Cultural Center 30–31
Near North Valley Neighborhood Association 33
Neri, San Felipe 15
New Mexico and Arizona Children's Home Society 116
New Mexico Bank & Trust 92–93
New Town 5, 11, 16, 17, 22, 24, 38, 39, 40, 44, 48, 49, 52, 58, 62, 108
Nick's restaurant 79
Nob Hill District 133, 135
Northeast Heights 65, 67, 87, 95, 113
N. T. Armijo Building 48
Nuestros Valores 27
Oak Street 122, 123
Occidental Life Building 82–83
Old Courthouse 24–25
Old Town 5, 11, 13, 14, 16, 17, 22, 24, 40, 48, 49, 52, 58, 62
Old Town Historical Society 11, 15
Orphanage 118–119
Otero, Miguel 72
Our Lady of the Angels School 10–11
Paris Shoe Store 74
Peck, Richard 127
Perea, Don José Leandro 38
Perkins Hall 108–109, 110, 124
Presbyterian Hospital 120–121, 123
Presbyterian Sanatorium 120–121, 122
President's House 126–127
Presley, Elvis 59
Public Service Company of New Mexico 77
Quarters restaurant 138
Quickel and Bothe's 56
Quizno's Subs 79
Railroad Avenue 38, 39, 40, 42, 44, 62, 88, 124
Railroad Depot 38–39
Raynolds, Joshua 109
Raynolds, Sarah 109
Regina Hall 118–119
Rio Grande 5, 14, 28, 34
Rio Grande Boulevard 14
Rio Grande Valley 5
Roosevelt, Franklin Delano 142
Rosenwald brothers 48
Rosenwald Building 78–79
Route 1 28
Route 66 5, 28, 29, 31, 92, 99, 112, 136, 137, 140
Roy E. Disney Center for Performing Arts 31
Rush, Olive 85
Sandia 5
Sandia Mountains 5, 58
Sandia School for Girls 21
San Felipe de Neri Church 6–7, 15, 24
San Felipe de Neri School 24–25
San Felipe Hotel 46–47
San Ignacio Chruch, Martineztown 34–35
San Mateo 134, 141
Santa Barbara 35, 36, 37
Santa Barbara Apartments 37
Santa Barbara School 36–37
Santa Fe 12, 29, 39, 63
Santa Fe Railroad 5, 43, 70, 92
Santa Fe Railroad Shops 102–103
Santa Fe Railroad Works 100–101
Sante Fe Trail 5, 10, 20

Second Street 50–51, 54, 55, 58, 80, 88
Segale, Sister Blandia 8, 9
Silver Avenue 62
Simmons, Marc 46, 104
Simms, Albert 69
Simms, John 69
Simms, Ruth Hanna McCormick 21
Simms Tower 68–69, 93
Sister Blandia Convent 8–9
Sixth Street 98
Skinner, A. J. 96
Skinner Building 96–97
South Fourth 31
South Valley 26, 29
Southwestern Brewery 104–105
Spencer, Francis W. 43
Springer Transfer Company building 39
Standard Diner 112–113
Steuckel-Johnson family 16
St. John's Episcopalian Cathedral 62–63
St. Joseph Hospital 114–115, 117, 119, 120
Stoney, James 63
Strong Building 81
Sturges Hotel 40, 41
St. Vincent's Academy 9, 11
Sulzer, J. F. 132
Sunnyside Inn 13
Sunshine Building 88–89
Telephone Pioneer Museum of New Mexico 73
Temple Albert 66–67
Third Street 44, 48–49, 52–53
Tight, William George 125
Tiguex 5
Tijeras Avenue 61
Tingley, Carrie 88, 142
Tingley, Charles 142
Tingley Beach Water Park 142–143
Triangle 130–131
Triangle Bar 130
Tricentennial Tiguex Park 18, 19
Trimble, W. L. 58
Trimble's 58–59
Trost, Henry C. 82, 89
Trujillo, Luisa de 20
University of New Mexico 124, 125, 126, 127, 128, 129
Valdés, Don Francisco Cuervo y 5, 6
Valentine Diners 131
Villa de Alburquerque 5
Villa di Capo 97
Walter G. Hope Building 52
Walter Street 35
Wells Fargo 50
West Bridge 31
Western Hardware 50
Wheels Museum 103
White Elephant Saloon 88
Whitney Hardware 41
Whittlesey, Charles 70
Winrock Mall 84
Wooster, Carrie 142
Wright, Charles 92, 93
Wright's Indian Trading Post 92–93
YMCA 36, 50
Yrisarri Building 78–79, 84
Zeiger, Charles 56
Zeiger Building 48, 56–57
Zimmerman, James 129
Zimmerman Library 128–129
Zuni 5